NorthStar

READING AND WRITING
High Intermediate

SECOND EDITION

Andrew K. English
Laura Monahon English

Series Editors
Frances Boyd
Carol Numrich

Longman

NorthStar: Reading and Writing, High Intermediate, Second Edition

Pearson Education, 10 Bank Street, White Plains, NY 10606

Development director: Penny Laporte
Project manager: Debbie Sistino
Development editor: Andrea Bryant
Vice president, director of design and production: Rhea Banker
Executive managing editor: Linda Moser
Associate production editor: Scott Fava
Production manager: Liza Pleva
Production coordinator: Melissa Leyva
Director of manufacturing: Patrice Fraccio
Senior manufacturing buyer: Dave Dickey
Photo research: Aerin Csigay
Cover design: Rhea Banker
Cover illustration: Detail of Der Rhein bei Duisburg, 1937, 145(R 5)
   Rhine near Duisburg 19 × 27.5 cm; water-based on cardboard;
   The Metropolitan Museum of Art, N.Y. The Berggruen Klee Collection,
   1984. (1984.315.56) Photograph © 1985 The Metropolitan Museum
   of Art. © 2003 Artists Rights Society (ARS), New York / VG
   Bild-Kunst, Bonn
Text design: Quorum Creative Services
Text composition: ElectraGraphics, Inc.
Text font: 11/13 Sabon
Text art: Duśan Petricic
Text credits: see page 245
Photo and art credits: see page 246

Der Rhein bei Duisburg
Paul Klee

Library of Congress Cataloging-in-Publication Data

English, Andrew K.
    NorthStar: Reading and writing, high intermediate / Andrew K.
English, Laura Monahon English.—2nd ed.
      p. cm.
    Includes index.
    ISBN 0-201-75573-4 (alk. paper)
    1. English language—Textbooks for foreign speakers. 2. Reading
comprehension—Problems, exercises, etc. 3. Report writing—
Problems, exercises, etc. I. Title: Reading and writing, high intermediate. II. English, Laura M. (Laura Monahon) III. Title

PE1128.E58   2004   97-43261
428.3'4—dc21   2003044479

0-201-75573-4 (Student Book)
0-13-184674-4 (Student Book with Audio CD)

1 2 3 4 5 6 7 8 9 10—CRK—09 08 07 06 05 04 03

To our parents, spouses, and son Sam,
whose love, support, and humor
made this all possible.

Contents

Welcome to *NorthStar,* Second Edition   vi

Scope and Sequence   xii

UNIT **1** Untruth and Consequences   1

UNIT **2** Dreams Never Die   23

UNIT **3** Dying for Their Beliefs   47

UNIT **4** When Disaster Strikes   67

UNIT **5** 21st-Century Living   87

UNIT **6** Give and Learn   111

UNIT **7** Homing in on Education   139

UNIT **8** Eat to Live or Live to Eat?   167

UNIT **9** The Grass Is Always Greener   193

UNIT **10** Take It or Leave It   217

Grammar Book References   243

Welcome to NorthStar

Second Edition

NorthStar leads the way in integrated skills series. The Second Edition remains an innovative, five-level series written for students with academic as well as personal language goals. Each unit of the thematically linked Reading and Writing strand and Listening and Speaking strand explores intellectually challenging, contemporary themes to stimulate critical thinking skills while building language competence.

Four easy to follow sections—Focus on the Topic, Focus on Reading/Focus on Listening, Focus on Vocabulary, and Focus on Writing/Focus on Speaking— invite students to focus on the process of learning through **NorthStar**.

Thematically Based Units

NorthStar engages students by organizing language study thematically. Themes provide stimulating topics for reading, writing, listening, and speaking.

From Advanced, Listening and Speaking

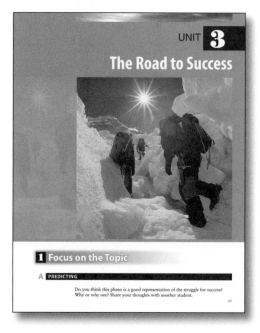

From Advanced, Reading and Writing

Extensive Support to Build Skills for Academic Success

Creative activities help students develop language-learning strategies, such as predicting and identifying main ideas and details.

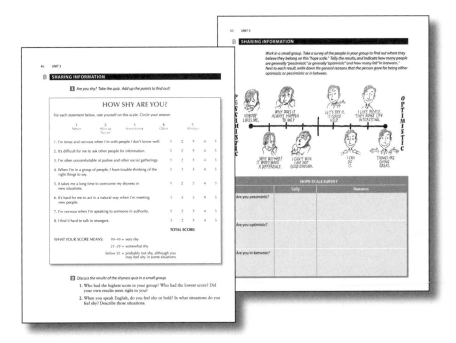

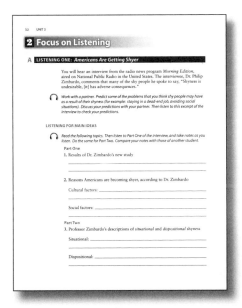

High-Interest Listening and Reading Selections

The two listening or reading selections in each unit present contrasting viewpoints to enrich students' understanding of the content while building language skills.

Critical Thinking Skill Development

Critical thinking skills, such as synthesizing information or reacting to the different viewpoints in the two reading or listening selections, are practiced throughout each unit, making language learning meaningful.

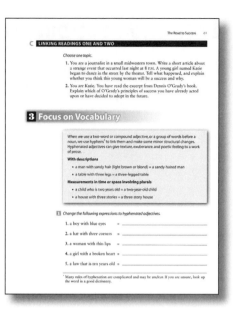

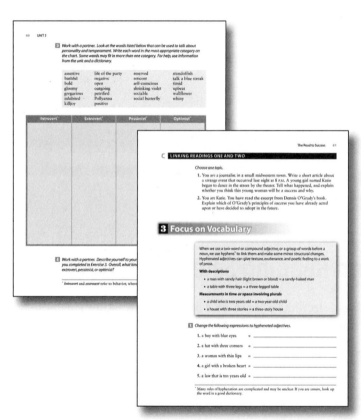

Extensive Vocabulary Practice

Students are introduced to key, contextualized vocabulary to help them comprehend the listening and reading selections. They also learn idioms, collocations, and word forms to help them explore, review, play with, and expand their spoken and written expression.

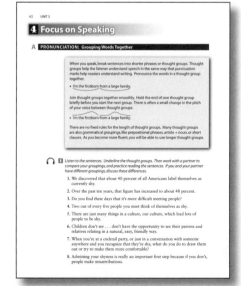

Powerful Pronunciation Practice

A carefully designed pronunciation syllabus in the Listening and Speaking strand focuses on topics such as stress, rhythm, and intonation. Theme-based pronunciation practice reinforces the vocabulary and content of the unit.

Content-Rich Grammar Practice

Each thematic unit integrates the study of grammar with related vocabulary and cultural information. The focus grammatical structures are drawn from the listening or reading selections and offer an opportunity for students to develop accuracy in speaking or writing about the topic.

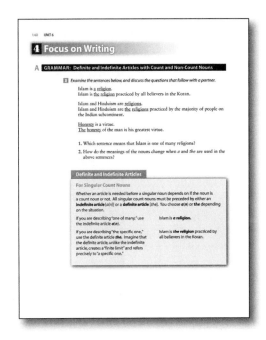

Extensive Opportunity for Discussion and Writing

Challenging and imaginative speaking activities, writing topics, and research assignments allow students to apply the language, grammar, style, and content they've learned.

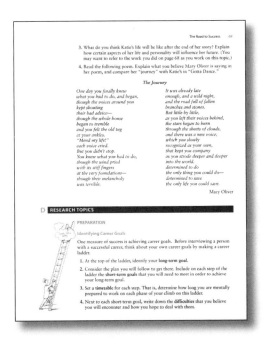

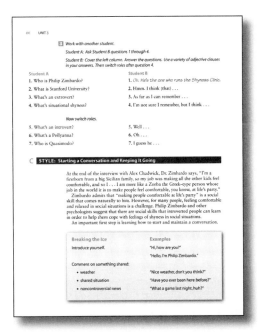

Writing Activity Book

The companion *Writing Activity Book* leads students through the writing process with engaging writing assignments. Skills and vocabulary from **NorthStar: Reading and Writing,** are reviewed and expanded as students learn the process of prewriting, organizing, revising, and editing.

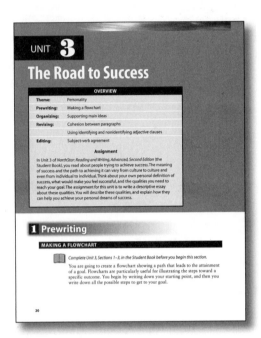

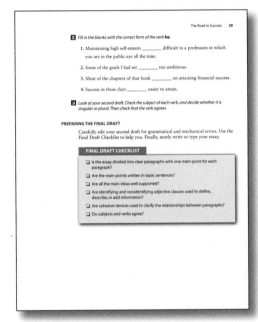

Audio Program

All the pronunciation, listening, and reading selections have been professionally recorded. The audio program includes audio CDs as well as audio cassettes.

Teacher's Manual with Achievement Tests

Each book in the series has an accompanying *Teacher's Manual* with step-by-step teaching suggestions, time guidelines, and expansion activities. Also included in each *Teacher's Manual* are reproducible unit-by-unit tests. The Listening and Speaking strand tests are recorded on CD and included in the *Teacher's Manual*. Packaged with each *Teacher's Manual* for the Reading and Writing strand is a CD-ROM that allows teachers to create and customize their own **NorthStar** tests. Answer Keys to both the Student Book and the Tests are included, along with a unit-by-unit word list of key vocabulary.

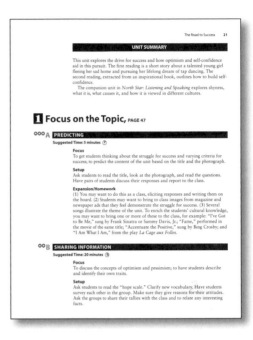

NorthStar Video Series

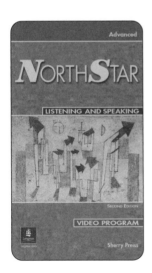

Engaging, authentic video clips, including cartoons, documentaries, interviews, and biographies correlate to the themes in **NorthStar.** There are four videos, one for each level of **NorthStar,** Second edition, containing 3- to 5- minute segments for each unit. Worksheets for the video can be found on the **NorthStar** Companion Website.

Companion Website

http://www.longman.com/northstar includes resources for students and teachers such as additional vocabulary activities, Web-based links and research, video worksheets, and correlations to state standards.

Scope and Sequence

Unit	Critical Thinking Skills	Reading Tasks

1
 	
Untruth and Consequences
 	
Theme: Media
 	
Reading One: *Peeping Tom Journalism*
  A media magazine article
 	
Reading Two: *Focus on Bomb Suspect Brings Tears and a Plea*
  A newspaper report
	Interpret a photograph
	Classify information
	Draw conclusions
	Hypothesize another point of view
		Interpret quotations
		Make predictions
		Analyze purpose of text
		Identify main ideas
		Scan for supporting details
		Identify author's viewpoint
		Research sensationalized news events
		Support answers with examples from the readings

2
 	
Dreams Never Die
 	
Theme: Overcoming Obstacles
 	
Reading One: *The Education of Frank McCourt*
  A biographical account
 	
Reading Two: *The Miracle: She altered our perception of the disabled and remapped the boundaries of sight and sense*
  A personal account
	Compare personal experiences
	Infer word meaning from context
	Interpret meaning of text
	Evaluate the role of obstacles and character in personal success
	Compare and contrast two life histories
	Interpret quotations
	Find correlations between two texts
		Make predictions
		Scan for information
		Identify chronology in a text
		Research a person who has overcome obstacles
		Support answers with information from the text

3
 	
Dying for Their Beliefs
 	
Theme: Medicine
 	
Reading One: *Dying for Their Beliefs: Christian Scientist Parents on Trial in Girl's Death*
  A newspaper report
 	
Reading Two: *Norman Cousins's Laugh Therapy*
  An expository account
	Compare and contrast two classes of medication
	Draw logical conclusions
	Re-evaluate assumptions in light of new information
	Analyze the development of an argument
		Make predictions
		Summarize main ideas
		Read for details
		Compare and contrast models from two texts
		Relate texts to personal values and experiences
		Use multiple sources to research medical treatments
		Support answers with information from the text
		Identify philosophical rationale for a text

4
 	
When Disaster Strikes
 	
Theme: Natural Disasters
 	
Reading One: *Drought*
  An eyewitness account
 	
Reading Two: *Monologue of Isabel Watching It Rain in Macondo*
  An excerpt from a novel
	Classify information
	Infer word meaning from context
	Analyze use of descriptive language in text
	Relate personal experiences to those of the author
	Interpret a character's emotions
		Read a graph
		Make predictions
		Identify chronology in a text
		Scan for supporting details
		Draw parallels between two different stories
		Locate specific words in the texts
		Use multiple sources to research a natural disaster

Writing Tasks	Vocabulary	Grammar
Develop topic sentences Write a letter to a newspaper editor Compose topic sentences with a controlling idea Edit topic sentences Write a paragraph presenting and supporting an opinion Brainstorm ideas using the web	Vocabulary categorization Word definitions Context clues Idiomatic expressions	Passive voice
Write a three-part paragraph with a topic sentence, supporting sentences, and a concluding sentence Edit out extraneous information in a paragraph Compose supporting sentences using transitional expressions Summarize research in a report	Synonyms Vocabulary categorization Context clues Idiomatic expressions	Gerunds and infinitives
Write an opinion essay Develop an opinion in outline form Compose questions with new vocabulary Support an opinion with evidence Develop a classroom survey Summarize research in a report	Vocabulary categorization Analogies Comparison and contrast of word meanings	Past unreal conditionals
Write a descriptive paragraph about a personal experience Write a paragraph that underscores similarities Use adjectives to compose descriptive sentences Write similes Write a descriptive essay Summarize research in a report that includes graphics and statistics	Synonyms Adjective suffixes Context clues Word associations Descriptive adjectives	Identifying adjective clauses

Unit	Critical Thinking Skills	Reading Tasks

5
21st Century Living
Theme: Conservation
Reading One: *Cities Against Nature*
    An excerpt from a textbook on urban planning
Reading Two: *Earthship Homes Catch Old Tires on Rebound*
    A newspaper report
	Interpret a photograph and drawing
	Compare observations on urban development
	Infer word meaning from context
	Extract logical arguments from the text to defend a position
	Classify information
	Evaluate benefits of environmental practices
	Identify language that denotes cause and effect
		Interpret a graph
		Paraphrase the main ideas
		Identify cause and effect in a text
		Identify connecting themes between texts
		Relate ideas in the texts to the local community
		Research an environmentally friendly project

6
Give and Learn
Theme: Philanthropy
Reading One: *Justin Lebo*
    An excerpt from a book on children activists
Reading Two: *Some Take the Time Gladly*
    A newspaper op-ed column
Mandatory Volunteering
    A newspaper op-ed column
	Re-evaluate personal attitudes and values
	Infer information not explicit in the text
	Identify an author's opinions
	Hypothesize another point of view
	Relate specific examples to broad themes
	Interpret quotations
		Make predictions
		Identify motivations of characters
		Paraphrase main ideas
		Scan for supporting details
		Identify contrasting arguments in the text
		Research community work

7
Homing in on Education
Theme: Education
Reading One: *Teaching at Home Hits New High with Internet*
    A newspaper report
Reading Two: *The Fun They Had*
    An excerpt from a science-fiction novel
	Re-evaluate personal assumptions
	Evaluate and classify information
	Compare and contrast models of education
	Infer information not explicit in the text
	Relate specific situations to broad themes
	Hypothesize another's point of view
	Analyze concessive language
		Read a bar graph
		Paraphrase main ideas in a reading
		Make predictions
		Summarize main ideas
		Identify main ideas and supporting details
		Research a home school organization

8
Eat to Live or Live to Eat?
Theme: Food
Reading One: *The Chinese Kitchen*
    A cook's narrative
Reading Two: *"Slow Food" Movement Aims at Restoring the Joy of Eating*
    A newspaper report
	Re-evaluate personal attitudes and values
	Compare and contrast information
	Infer meaning not explicit in the text
	Identify different perspectives within one text
	Analyze techniques in narrative voice
	Identify connecting themes between texts
		Make predictions
		Restate main ideas
		Locate specific information in the text
		Relate the text to personal culinary experiences
		Support opinions with information from the text

Writing Tasks	Vocabulary	Grammar
Develop an urban land use plan Write a paragraph response using new vocabulary Write cause and effect sentences Use subordinating conjunctions and transitions to express cause and effect Write a cause-and-effect essay Summarize research in a report	Synonyms Context clues Word forms	Advisability and obligation in the past
Use commas, semicolons, colons, and dashes Express an opinion in a letter Write free responses using new vocabulary Write an essay Take notes on research using graphic organizer Summarize research in a report	Synonyms Word classification Word forms Phrasal verbs Context clues Word definitions	Tag questions
Write an opinion essay Take notes on a reading Write sentences interpreting characters using new vocabulary Write opinion statements that make concessions to other points of views Write sentences using dependent clauses Write an outline for a group report	Synonyms Context clues Dialect variations in spelling Word forms	Direct and indirect speech
Write a narrative Evaluate a classmate's narrative using a rubric Practice parallel structures and sentence variation Organize information in a narrative Write interview questions	Context clues Synonyms Adverbs Idiomatic expressions Phrasal verbs	Phrasal verbs

Unit	Critical Thinking Skills	Reading Tasks

9
 	
The Grass Is Always Greener
 	
Theme: Immigration
 	
Reading One: *Poor Visitor*
   An immigrant's narrative
 	
Reading Two: *Nostalgia*
   A poem
	Classify observations and life experience
	Identify similarities in three different life histories
	Interpret imagery in text
	Compare and contrast imagery in text
	Hypothesize another's point of view
		Scan for information
		Identify connecting themes in two texts
		Paraphrase main ideas
		Relate text to personal experiences
		Read a time line
		Research the life of an immigrant
		Support answers with information from the text

10
 	
Take It or Leave It
 	
Theme: Technology
 	
Reading One: *Inside the House*
   An excerpt from a book on technology
 	
Reading Two: *Thoreau's Home*
   An excerpt from *Walden*
	Compare and contrast concepts of technology
	Evaluate personal standards in technology
	Infer word meaning from context
	Support inferences with examples from the text
	Hypothesize another point of view
	Classify information in a text
	Interpret a cartoon
		Make predictions
		Identify main ideas
		Locate examples and details in a text
		Recognize organization of a text
		Relate text to personal values

Writing Tasks	Vocabulary	Grammar
Write a compare and contrast essay Use transitional expressions and subordinating conjunctions to combine sentences Write compare and contrast statements Edit a letter Write a report on research Generate descriptive words	Multiple definitions of words Context clues Vocabulary categorization Analogies	Past perfect Time words
Take notes in outline form Develop an essay from an outline Compose open responses using new vocabulary Brainstorm ideas using a graphic organizer Write interview questions Report on an interview	Synonyms Context clues Word forms	Future progressive Time clauses

Acknowledgments

We would like to express our gratitude and thanks to the entire NorthStar team of authors, editors, and assistants. Special thanks go to Carol Numrich and Frances Boyd for their vision, ideas, and guidance. We are, as always, honored to be on their team. Thanks also to Andrea Bryant for her unending support and attention to detail. To everyone else at Pearson, many thanks for all of your hard work in bringing this second edition to fruition.

Untruth and Consequences

1 Focus on the Topic

A PREDICTING

Look at the photograph of Princess Diana and the title of the unit. Then discuss these questions with a partner.

1. What is happening? What do you think the photographer is thinking? What do you think Princess Diana is thinking?

2. Where do most people learn about news? What news source do you most frequently use—newspapers, magazines, television, radio, the Internet? Why?

3. What do you think the title of the unit means? What do you think this unit will be about?

B   SHARING INFORMATION

Work in a small group. Circle the letter of the best interpretations for quotations 1 and 2. Then write your own interpretation of quotations 3 and 4. Discuss your answers. Do you agree with any of these quotations? Why or why not?

1. "When a dog bites a man, that is not news; but when a man bites a dog, that is news."   —Leo Rosten, political scientist and author

   a. News is only about exciting or unusual events.

   b. News is only interesting when someone gets hurt.

2. "A dog fight in Brooklyn [New York] is bigger than a revolution in China."
                                                    —*Brooklyn Eagle* (newspaper)

   a. News about the United States is always more newsworthy than international news.

   b. People are more interested in local news than international news even when the international news is more newsworthy.

3. "Good news isn't news. Bad news is news."
                                                    —Henry Luce, founder of *Time* (magazine)

   This means: _____

   _____

4. "What is news? You know what news is? News is what (you) news directors interpret it as. News is what we at CNN interpret it as. The people of this country see the news that we think they ought to see. And quite frankly, a lot of that decision is geared to what's going to keep them interested, keep them at your station."

                                                    —Ted Turner, founder of CNN
                                                    (Cable News Network)

   This means: _____

   _____

C   PREPARING TO READ

BACKGROUND

News is everywhere and serves many different functions. The news gives instant coverage of important events. News also provides facts and information. In addition, news is business—a way to make money by selling advertising and/or newspapers and magazines. Sometimes news is manipulated by the government as a way to control a population. Whatever news is, it is all around us. You can't escape it. Every day we are bombarded by information from newspapers, magazines, television, and the Internet.

"News" does not always mean something that is unquestionably true. Although the news *seems* to be based on facts, these facts are interpreted and reported the way the media chooses to report them. For example, some information that appears as news is really only speculation,[1] or theories formed by the reporters. Furthermore, many journalists and reporters sensationalize or dramatize a news event in order to make a story more interesting. Unfortunately, sensationalism often stretches the truth and hurts the people it involves. Therefore, as consumers of news we must learn to think critically about the news, the media, and what the truth is.

The news functions in many different ways. Match the following newspaper items with their function (as described above).

FUNCTION		NEWSPAPER ITEM
___ 1. give instant coverage to important events	a.	Today's weather will be sunny and calm. Temperatures will be in the 80s.
___ 2. provide facts	b.	Movie star Glenda Moon was seen yesterday shopping in a local jewelry store with an unidentified man. Salespeople refused to answer questions, but one customer said they were looking at diamond rings. Could a wedding be in her future?
___ 3. make money for the newspaper	c.	One-day sale at Marty's! Bring in your store coupons and receive an additional 15% off any sale item!
___ 4. manipulate information	d.	Senator Hoffman died in his sleep early this morning. The cause of death is unknown. More information is expected to come later today.
___ 5. sensationalize events	e.	The government says the country's army is now the strongest and best equipped in the world. Despite last month's report stating that our military technology was outdated, the military assures us our country is the safest it has ever been.

---

[1] *speculation:* assumptions

VOCABULARY FOR COMPREHENSION

Work with a partner and discuss the meaning of the vocabulary words. Use a dictionary if you need help. Then check (✓) the category or categories you associate with each word.

VOCABULARY WORDS	PRINT MEDIA (Newspapers, Magazines, Internet)	TELEVISION AND RADIO
reporter	✓	✓
affiliate		
anchor		
celebrity		
columnist		
correspondent		
editor		
journalist		
network		
politician		
tabloid		

2 Focus on Reading

A READING ONE: *Peeping Tom Journalism*

Read the first three paragraphs of "Peeping Tom Journalism." Work with a partner to answer the questions in paragraph 3. Then read the rest of the article.

PEEPING TOM[1] JOURNALISM

BY NANCY DAY
(from *Sensational TV—Trash or Journalism*)

1   Reporters constantly struggle with what and how much to tell. Sometimes the facts are clear. Other times, journalists must rely on their own judgment.

2   A retired minister[2] in a small town does not return from a fishing trip. Police find his car parked about halfway to the lake. It is locked and undamaged. In it they find a half-eaten ham sandwich, fishing tackle, a gun with one shell fired, and a copy of *Penthouse* (a magazine that contains pictures of naked women). The minister is missing. You're the reporter and your story is due.

3   What do you report? Suppose the minister just went for a walk? Do you risk embarrassment and mention the magazine? Is the gun important? Should you propose any theories about what might have happened?

4   The reporter who actually faced these decisions decided to mention the gun, the sandwich, the fishing tackle, and the condition of the car, but not the magazine or any speculation. The minister's body was later found. He had been killed by a hitchhiker, who had left the magazine in the minister's car.

5   In the old days, reporters knew politicians (including presidents) who slept around, movie stars who were gay, and public figures who used drugs or abused alcohol. They just kept it to themselves. Now, at least in part because the public seems to have an endless hunger for it, reporters sometimes cover these aspects of celebrities' lives more than any other.

6   Some of the interest can be justified on the basis that character affects how people perform their jobs. But what if the information isn't relevant? For example, does the public need to know that a senator is gay? When a famous person dies, does the public have a right to all the details? Should

---

[1] *Peeping Tom:* a person who secretly watches others
[2] *minister:* a person who performs religious functions in a Protestant church

the public know which public figures are unfaithful to their spouses? Are these things we need to know or just things we want to know?

7   When Gennifer Flowers alleged a twelve-year affair with President Bill Clinton, she first sold the story to the tabloid *Star.* CNN reported the story and so did the networks and the major newspapers and news magazines. Peter Jennings, anchor for ABC's[3] "World News Tonight," was against broadcasting the Flowers story without further reporting by ABC correspondents, but says, "it was made clear to [me] . . . that if you didn't go with the story, every [ABC] affiliate in the country would look up and say, 'What the hell's going on in this place? Don't they know a story when they see it?'"

8   Some stories receive such wide visibility that to ignore them is to "play ostrich man," says Shelby Coffey, editor of the *Los Angeles Times.* "You have to give your readers some perspective on the information they are getting."

9   Scrutiny[4] may be the price one pays for fame. But what about relatives of celebrities? Are they fair game too? And what about the average person?

10   When Sara Jane Moore pointed a gun at President Ford,[5] a man in the crowd knocked her hand, deflecting the shot. The man, Oliver W. Sipple, became an instant hero. He was thirty-three years old and a Marine veteran. What else did the public want or need to know about him? Initial reports did not mention Sipple's sexual orientation. But when a San Francisco news columnist said that local gay leaders were proud of Sipple's actions, other papers began to report it. Sipple sued the columnist and several newspapers for invading his privacy. He said that he suffered "great mental anguish, embarrassment and humiliation." Lawyers argued that by becoming involved in an event of worldwide importance, Sipple had given up his right to privacy because the public has a legitimate interest in his activity.

11   Rosa Lopez was a maid working quietly and anonymously[6] until she became a key witness in the O. J. Simpson trial.[7] Suddenly, she was the focus of intense scrutiny. Lopez was hounded by cameras and reporters everywhere she went. Her every move was analyzed. She eventually returned to her native country to escape the pressure, only to find that the media followed her there.

12   How many witnesses will come forward in the future, knowing what kind of treatment awaits them? Do people who accidentally find themselves involved in such high-profile cases have rights, or do we deserve to know everything about them?

---

[3] *ABC:* American Broadcasting Companies, Inc.; a major television network in the United States
[4] *scrutiny:* the process of examining something closely and carefully
[5] *President Ford:* Gerald Ford, the 38th President of the United States (1974–1977)
[6] *anonymously:* namelessly, in secret
[7] O. J. Simpson is a famous former football player, actor, and sportscaster who was accused of killing his ex-wife and a male friend of hers. His trial was followed closely by the media. He eventually was found not guilty in criminal court but guilty in civil court.

READING FOR MAIN IDEAS

Reading One can be divided into four main ideas. What does the reading say about each idea? Circle the letter of the sentence that best summarizes the idea.

1. Reporting of facts
   a. Journalists sometimes use their own judgment and leave out certain facts when reporting a story.
   b. Journalists usually report all the facts that they know about a story.

2. Reporting about famous people
   a. In the old days, certain facts about celebrities and other famous people were held back from the public. This is not always the case today.
   b. In the old days, certain facts about celebrities and other famous people were held back from the public. This is still the case today.

3. Choosing to report all stories
   a. The decision to report or not report a story is based only on the reporter's judgment.
   b. The decision to report or not report a story is influenced by many factors. The reporter's judgment is just one of these factors.

4. Respecting the right to privacy
   a. All people agree that the public has a right to know about a famous person's life.
   b. Some people believe that you lose the right to privacy when you are famous. Others disagree.

READING FOR DETAILS

Complete the chart with examples or details the author uses to support each of the main ideas.

MAIN IDEA	EXAMPLE THAT SUPPORTS THE MAIN IDEA
1. Reporting of facts	*Case of the retired minister*
2. Reporting about famous people	
3. Choosing to report all stories	
4. Respecting the right to privacy	

REACTING TO THE READING

1 *The reading raises some interesting questions about one's right to privacy. Read the following statements and check (✓) whether you think the author would agree or disagree. Then write the number of the paragraph where you found your information. (Note that the author does not actually state her opinion directly, but through careful reading you can infer what her opinion is.) When you are finished, discuss your answers with a partner. If necessary, refer back to the reading to support your answers.*

1. The public has the right to know about the sexual behavior of politicians.

   author agrees _____   author disagrees _____   paragraph _____

2. When a famous person dies, the public has a right to know all the details of the person's life and death.

   author agrees _____   author disagrees _____   paragraph _____

3. The public should know which public figures are unfaithful to their spouses.

   author agrees _____   author disagrees _____   paragraph _____

4. An average person who suddenly becomes the focus of unwanted media attention has no right to privacy.

   author agrees _____   author disagrees _____   paragraph _____

5. It was easier to be a reporter in "the old days."

   author agrees _____   author disagrees _____   paragraph _____

6. The Gennifer Flowers story should not have been covered by CNN and the other major networks.

   author agrees _____   author disagrees _____   paragraph _____

2 *Throughout Reading One, the author asks the reader various questions. With a partner, answer the following questions. Then share your answers with the class.*

1. Does the public need to know a senator's sexual orientation? When a famous person dies, does the public have a right to all the details? Should the public know which public figures are unfaithful to their spouses? Are these things we need to know or just things we want to know?

2. Scrutiny may be the price one pays for fame. But what about relatives of celebrities? Are they fair game too? And what about the average person?

3. How many witnesses will come forward in the future (in high-profile cases), knowing what kind of treatment awaits them? Do people who accidentally find themselves involved in such high-profile cases have rights, or do we deserve to know everything about them?

B   READING TWO: *Focus on Bomb Suspect Brings Tears and a Plea*

On July 27, 1996, during one of the first evening celebrations held at the Olympics in Atlanta, Georgia, a bomb exploded in Centennial Olympic Park. The bomb killed one person and injured 111 others. Richard Jewell, a security guard at the park who discovered the bomb and helped numerous people to safety, was first considered a hero of the tragic incident. Later he was accused of putting the bomb there. The media then surrounded him and scrutinized his every action—past and present. They left nothing about his personal life untouched. He was later cleared of any suspicions, but his life has never been the same.

Discuss these questions in a small group.

1. How do you think Richard Jewell's life changed initially after he discovered the bomb?

2. How do you think Richard Jewell's life changed after he was accused?

3. How did the media's scrutiny affect his daily life?

Focus on Bomb Suspect Brings Tears and a Plea

By Rick Bragg (from the *New York Times*)

1   Barbara Jewell stared into the unblinking eyes of the television cameras she has come to despise and spoke in tears today of how life had changed for her son, Richard, since he was named a month ago as a suspect in the bombing in Centennial Olympic Park.[1] "Now my son has no real life," said Mrs. Jewell, a little gray-haired woman, speaking out for the first time since her 33-year-old son was suspected—but never arrested or charged—in the bombing that killed one person and injured 111 others.

2   "He is a prisoner in my home," Mrs. Jewell said at a news conference this afternoon. "He cannot work. He cannot know any type of normal life. He can only sit and wait for this nightmare to end."

3   She begged President Clinton to clear her son's name and asked reporters to spread the word that her son was innocent of any wrongdoing in the July 27 bombing. After her tearful request, her son's lawyers said they would file civil lawsuits over reporting on the case.

Richard Jewell

[1] *Centennial Olympic Park:* a large park and central meeting place located in Atlanta, Georgia, site of the 1996 Summer Olympic Games

4   Richard A. Jewell, a security guard in Centennial Olympic Park and a former sheriff's deputy,[2] was at first hailed as a hero for discovering the bomb and helping to clear people from the area. Then news accounts, including a special edition of the *Atlanta Journal*,[3] named him as a suspect. Since then, television and news executives have repeatedly debated the intense attention focused on Mr. Jewell, with most deciding that too many people knew he was a suspect for his name to be avoided or suppressed.

5   "Last week, a close family friend of twenty-nine years took seriously ill," Mrs. Jewell said. "While he was on his deathbed, because Richard did not want to subject him to the world attention of the media, he did not go see him. Richard was not able to see his friend before he died." Her son did go to the funeral home after his friend died, she said. "When we returned from the funeral home, for the first time I saw my son sobbing," Mrs. Jewell said, breaking into tears herself as she recounted the story. He said, "Mama, everybody was looking."

6   "I do not think any of you can even begin to imagine what our lives are like. Richard is not a murderer," said Mrs. Jewell, an insurance claims coordinator. But, she said, "He has been convicted in the court of public opinion."

7   Meanwhile, the Jewells continue to be besieged by reporters. "They have taken all privacy from us," Mrs. Jewell said. "They have taken all peace. They have rented an apartment which faces our home in order to keep their cameras trained on us around the clock. They watch and photograph everything we do. We wake up to photographers, we go to sleep with photographers. We cannot look out the windows. We cannot walk our dogs without being followed down the sidewalk."

8   Mrs. Jewell said she was not just saddened and hurt by the ordeal, but was also angry.

[2] *sheriff's deputy:* law officer
[3] *Atlanta Journal:* a newspaper

Complete the chart with information about how Richard Jewell's life changed after he was named a suspect in the bombing.

BEFORE THE BOMBING	AFTER THE BOMBING
1. Worked as a security guard	
2. Visited friends	
3. Went out; walked his dogs	
4. Had a private life	

C LINKING READINGS ONE AND TWO

Imagine you are Barbara Jewell. Complete the following letter to the Atlanta Journal, *the newspaper that first named your son as a suspect in the Olympic bombing. In the letter, say that you are angry that your son was named as a suspect and explain how your lives have changed because of it. Address the issue of a person's right to privacy. Use Rosa Lopez and Oliver Sipple from Reading One as examples of others whose lives the media has damaged.*

To the Editor:

    Sensationalist reporting is harmful to all people involved and has no place in our society.

_____

_____

_____

_____

_____

_____

_____

_____

_____

_____

_____

_____

_____

_____

    As a result of the media's tolerance for irresponsible reporting, my family and I are a few more victims of sensationalism at its worst. On behalf of all victims of sensationalism, we demand a formal apology.

Barbara Jewell

3 Focus on Vocabulary

1 *You know you are reading an idiom when you understand each separate word in an expression, but not the expression as a whole. An idiom is a group of words with a different meaning from the separate words. Work in a small group. Read the following sentences and circle the letter of the best explanation for each underlined idiom.*

1. In the old days, reporters <u>kept</u> some information about politicians and movie stars <u>to themselves</u>.
   a. didn't talk about something
   b. made a promise
   c. cared for oneself

2. Now, at least in part because the public seems to <u>have an endless hunger for</u> it, reporters sometimes cover these aspects of celebrities' lives more than any other.
   a. need to constantly eat
   b. have continual need for something
   c. dislike something immensely

3. Some stories receive such wide visibility that to ignore them is to "<u>play ostrich man</u>," says Shelby Coffey, editor of the *Los Angeles Times*.
   a. wear a special bird costume
   b. try to find the truth in something
   c. ignore something that is obvious

4. Scrutiny may be <u>the price one pays</u> for fame.
   a. suffering for your actions
   b. buying something you can't afford
   c. paying too much money for something

5. But what about relatives of celebrities? Are they <u>fair game</u>, too?
   a. victims of sensational writing
   b. someone that you can criticize or attack
   c. a game that is played at a fair or festival

6. Lopez was <u>hounded</u> by cameras and reporters everywhere she went.
   a. found
   b. followed
   c. treated like a dog

7. She begged President Clinton to clear her son's name and asked reporters to <u>spread the word</u> that her son was innocent of any wrongdoing.
   a. hide the fact
   b. stop reporting
   c. tell everyone

8. Even though Richard Jewell's friend was <u>on his deathbed</u>, Richard didn't visit him.
   a. in the bed you have chosen to die in
   b. extremely sick, dying
   c. in a very deep sleep

9. "Richard is not a murderer," said Mrs. Jewell, but "he has been <u>convicted in the court of public opinion</u>."
   a. considered guilty by everyone before going to trial
   b. in a special trial in which you are found guilty
   c. forced to take part in a trial as a member of the jury

10. Reporters watched the Jewell family <u>around the clock</u>.
   a. from sunrise to sunset
   b. twenty-four hours a day
   c. during the night

2 *Work in a small group or with a partner. Decide which of the following people could have made the statements listed below. Write the appropriate letter in the space next to each statement. In some cases, more than one person could have made the statement. Refer to the readings to support your answers.*

a. Gennifer Flowers, woman alleged to have had an affair with President Clinton

b. Reporter of the minister story

c. Shelby Coffey, editor of the *Los Angeles Times*

d. Peter Jennings, ABC News anchor

e. Rosa Lopez, key witness in the O. J. Simpson trial

f. Richard Jewell, man accused of the Olympic Park bombing

_____ 1. The public seems to have an endless hunger for news, and it is our responsibility to provide information to the readers so they can form their own opinions.

_____ 2. I want the public to know about my life; if the president wants to keep his private life to himself, that's his business.

_____ 3. The media can ruin your life. Reporters have no right to invade my privacy by hounding me around the clock.

_____ 4. Even though there are some stories I would rather not report, I can't play ostrich man all the time.

_____ 5. I'm glad I waited to report all the facts, because some of them might have been misinterpreted. I don't want anyone to be convicted wrongly in the court of public opinion.

_____ 6. Just because I'm a small part of a news story does not mean that unrelated parts of my life are fair game for reporters to write about.

3 *Write a response to this reporter. Use at least five of the idioms in the box.*

> I know everyone thinks reporters are sensationalist and responsible for ruining people's lives. However, if we don't report everything, and quickly, someone else will. Then my boss will want to know why our paper didn't get the story. In fact, I could lose my job!

keep something to oneself	pay the price
have an endless hunger for	be hounded
be on one's deathbed	spread the word
around the clock	play ostrich man
be convicted in the court of public opinion	fair game

4 Focus on Writing

A   GRAMMAR: Passive Voice

1 *Examine the following sets of sentences and answer the questions with a partner.*

Passive Voice

- The minister had been killed by a hitchhiker.

- Rosa Lopez was hounded by cameras and reporters everywhere she went.

- At first, Richard Jewell was hailed as a hero (by people).

Active Voice

- A hitchhiker had killed the minister.

- Cameras and reporters hounded Rosa Lopez everywhere she went.

- At first, people hailed Richard Jewell as a hero.

1. The sentences in each pair have a different grammar structure, but the same meaning. What is the grammar structure in the passive sentences? What is the structure in the active sentences?

_____

_____

2. List the words in the subject position in the passive sentences.

_____   _____   _____

3. List the words in the subject position in the active sentences.

_____   _____   _____

4. The difference in subject between an active and a passive sentence shows a change in the focus of the sentence. In the examples above, the active sentences seem to focus on _a hitchhiker, cameras and reporters_, and _people_. The subject in these sentences performs the action. What seems to be the focus of the passive sentences? Do the words in the subject position in these sentences perform the action?

_____

_____

Passive Voice

Forming the Passive Voice

To form the **passive voice,** use the correct form of **be** + past participle. At times, the person or thing (the agent) responsible for doing the action is used. In this case, use **by** + the name of the agent:

Subject Position	Be	Past Participle	(By + Agent)
Rosa Lopez	is	hounded	by cameras and reporters.
Rosa Lopez	was	hounded	by cameras and reporters.
Rosa Lopez	has been	hounded	by cameras and reporters.

Using the Passive Voice

1. Active sentences focus on the person or thing that performs an action. **Passive sentences** focus on the person or thing that receives or is the result of an action. The meaning of passive and active sentences is usually similar, but the focus changes.

(continued)

Active	Passive
A hitchhiker had killed the minister.	The minister had been killed by a hitchhiker.
(The hitchhiker is the focus of the sentence.)	(The minister is the focus of the sentence.)

2. Use the passive voice **without an agent** (the person or thing performing the action) when:

a. the person (agent) is unknown or unimportant

"The minister's body **was** later **found.**" (You don't know who found the body; it doesn't matter who found the body. What is important is that someone, anyone, found the body.)

b. the person (agent) is understood from the context

"It **was made clear** to Peter Jennings that he had to go with the story." (It is understood that a superior, probably his boss, made it clear to him.)

c. you want to avoid mentioning the person (agent) responsible

"The FBI said the Richard Jewell investigation **was carried out** incorrectly." (The FBI does not want to name exactly who in the FBI made mistakes during the investigation.)

3. Use the passive voice **with an agent** (*by* + **noun**) when:

a. you want to make the receiver of the action more important than the one who performs the action

"Lopez **was hounded** by cameras and reporters everywhere she went." (Lopez is the focus of the sentence. She is more important than the cameras and reporters that hounded her.)

b. the information is necessary to complete the meaning, or when it is new or surprising information

"Focus on Bomb Suspect Brings Tears and a Plea" **was written** by Rick Bragg.

2 *Complete the following sentences. Use the active or passive voice in the past tense.*

1. The news columnist ___reported___ on all aspects of Oliver Sipple's
   (report)
   life, not only those related to his act of heroism.

2. The Gennifer Flowers story _____ on all the major TV
   (broadcast)
   networks.

3. Some of the interest in the lives of politicians _____ on the
   (justify)
   basis that character affects how people perform their jobs.

4. The retired minister _____ from his fishing trip.
   (not return)

5. A half-eaten ham sandwich, a gun, fishing tackle, and a magazine

   _____ in the minister's car.
   (find)

6. The reporter who wrote the story about the minister _____ to
   (decide)
   mention the gun and the sandwich, but not the magazine.

7. The reporter's story _____ by many people, including the
   (read)
   minister's relatives.

8. Sara Jane Moore _____ a gun at President Ford.
   (point)

9. The shot _____ when Oliver W. Sipple knocked her hand.
   (deflect)

10. Witnesses _____ about the shooting by the police.
    (question)

3 *Complete the following sentences. Use the passive voice in the past tense. Include the agent only if it is necessary information.*

1. The local police force worked hard. The investigation

   ___was completed___ in less than 72 hours.
   (complete/police)

2. Richard Jewell _____ about where he saw the package
   (interview/FBI)
   containing the bomb and why he suspected that it contained a bomb.

3. The news was interrupted to report that the president

   _____ .
   (shoot/an assassin)

4. Richard Jewell's mother felt Richard _____ before he

(convict/media)

even went to trial.

5. The celebrity _____ today at 5:00 P.M.

(marry/a minister)

6. The newspaper story, which _____ , talks about the

(write/Peter Jennings)

responsibility of the media in reporting the news.

7. The defendant, a news reporter, _____ of character

(find guilty/a jury)

defamation after a three-week-long jury trial.

B   STYLE: Topic Sentences

1 *Examine this paragraph and discuss the questions with the class.*

News is everywhere and serves many different functions. The news gives
instant coverage of important events. News also provides facts and information.
In addition, news is business—a way to make money by selling advertising
and/or newspapers and magazines. Sometimes news is manipulated by the
government as a way to control a population. Whatever news is, it is all around
us. You can't escape it. Every day we are bombarded by information from
newspapers, magazines, television, and the Internet.

1. What is the topic of this paragraph?

2. The first sentence is the topic sentence. What two ideas are presented in this
sentence?

3. How does the content of the rest of the paragraph relate to the topic sentence?

Topic Sentences

The **topic sentence** is an essential part of a well-written paragraph. The topic
sentence controls the content of the rest of the paragraph. This control helps the
writer focus on supporting ideas in the paragraph that are directly related to the
topic sentence. The first step in writing a topic sentence is to choose a topic and
find a point of view or main idea about it. For example:

Topic	Main Idea
news	News is everywhere.
television	Television is a bad influence.
reading	Reading is good for you.

The next step is to narrow the main idea even more by finding a controlling idea. The **controlling idea** is the idea you want to explain, illustrate, or describe in the paragraph. It makes a specific statement about a topic. The controlling ideas in the following topic sentences are underlined.

Main Idea	Main Idea + <u>Controlling Idea</u> = Topic Sentence
news is everywhere	News is everywhere and <u>serves many different functions</u>.
television is bad	Television has a <u>violent influence on children</u>.
reading is good	Reading helps you <u>expand your mind and broaden your interests</u>.

2 *Each of the following paragraphs is missing a topic sentence. Circle the letter of the topic sentence that best fits the paragraph. Discuss your answers with a partner.*

1. For example, you can't pick up a newspaper these days without reading about some outrageous or gruesome crime. The top television news story is usually about a murder or other violent incident. We need to read and hear about the good news stories, too. Otherwise, we will continue sending the message that only violence is worth reporting. What kind of message is that for our children?

   a. Our society is becoming more and more violent every day.
   b. Television news coverage focuses only on violent news.
   c. All of the media have become increasingly negative by focusing only on violence.

2. As a result of live television, people can receive news as it happens. For example, during the September 11 attack on the World Trade Center in New York City, CNN viewers could see the second plane hit as the news was covering the first plane's attack. Because of "live" reporting, people feel as though they are participating in history, not just reading or hearing about it afterwards. It has changed the viewer's role completely.

   a. These days, there is more live television coverage than ever before.
   b. "Live" television reporting has changed the way we see the news.
   c. CNN changed the way we saw the news during the September 11 attacks.

3. Experts recommend limiting viewing to one hour per day during the week and up to two hours per day on weekends. The programs should be educational in content and promote discussion between the parent and child. Programs on animal behavior and family values, and programs that teach basic learning skills, are highly recommended.

   a. Watching television is not bad for children and it's fine for teenagers and adults, too.
   b. Watching television is fine for children as long as you limit the hours and monitor the programs.
   c. Programs for children should be educational in content so that the time spent watching TV is not wasted.

4. What we see on the nightly news has been carefully selected by the news department at the television station. Because the station is interested in making money, the news that is selected is not necessarily the most important news but rather the news that will attract the most viewers. As a result, we only see the news that has been chosen for us, which is not always the most informative.

    a. It is very important that the news make money.
    b. The news director selects the news with the help of reporters.
    c. News is not simply what we see, but what the news director at the television station wants us to see.

3 *The topic sentences in the following paragraphs are underlined. They are incomplete because they do not have a controlling idea. Rewrite each topic sentence, using a topic and a controlling idea.*

1. <u>Celebrities have jobs</u>. Being a movie star or sports star is their job. It is what they are good at. They should not be under the continual scrutiny of the media just because of their profession. They have a right to a private life just like you and I.

    Rewrite: *Celebrities deserve private lives like any other person.*

2. <u>News is different</u>. In the old days, people got their news by word of mouth. As society became more literate and printing costs decreased, newspapers became the medium. Radio then brought a sense of immediacy to the news. Television added the visual impact. Now we have the Internet, which gives up-to-the-second news about any news event any time we want it. Who knows what the news medium of the future will be?

    Rewrite: _____

3. <u>Politicians are public figures</u>. As a president, one is supposed to represent the qualities of honesty and integrity. Remaining faithful to your husband or wife is the purest example of these qualities. If a president is unfaithful to his or her spouse, how can we trust that he or she is honest in handling presidential duties? Therefore, the media have the responsibility to inform us when a public figure is unfaithful.

    Rewrite: _____

4. <u>Reading is hard</u>. As with any program of exercise, you have to discipline yourself and make reading the newspaper a part of your everyday routine. And just as exercise makes your body stronger, reading makes your mind stronger. It broadens your interests, gives you the ability to think critically about important issues, and enables you to participate in interesting conversations. In conclusion, reading the paper, like any exercise, is time well spent.

    Rewrite: _____

C WRITING TOPICS

Write a paragraph about one of these topics. Be sure to use some of the ideas, vocabulary, grammar, and style that you have learned in this unit.

1. Does sensational news ever have a place in our society? If yes, be specific and describe when and in what place. If no, be specific and explain why not.

2. How can the media influence or shape a society's values? Be specific and give examples.

3. Do governments have the right to censor television programs (for sexual content and violence, for example)? Be specific and explain why or why not.

4. Do the media reflect society, or does society reflect the media? Be specific and give examples.

D RESEARCH TOPICS

1 *Work in a small group. Think about news events in the past or present when you felt the media (television, print, or the Internet) sensationalized the reporting of a story and caused anguish or embarrassment to the person(s) involved. Discuss how the media sensationalized the story and how they should have covered the story instead. Take notes below and share your examples with the class.*

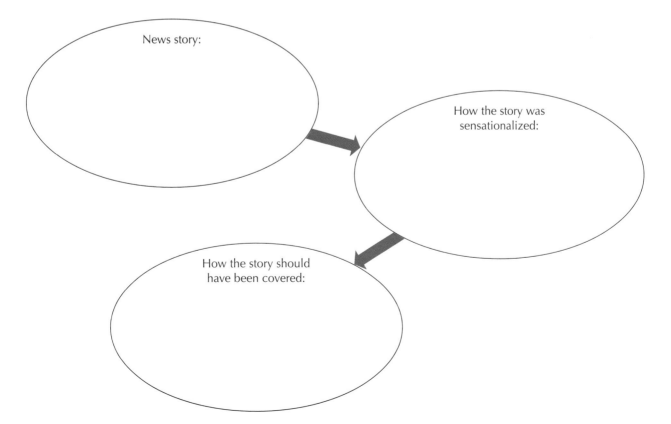

News story:

How the story was sensationalized:

How the story should have been covered:

2 *Over the course of a few days, find examples of sensationalized news events from newspapers, magazines, television news programs, or websites. Then find articles about the same story covered by different news sources. Compare the information in the different sources. Bring the articles to class and discuss them in small groups. Write the answers to the following questions about each story and present to another group.*

- Is there any difference in the information presented in each news source? What are the differences? Which source do you feel covered the story best? Why?

- How was the story sensationalized?

- Why do you think the media covered this story?

- What does the media think you want to know about this story?

- Does the focus of the story change the way you feel about the news event or the people involved in the event? If so, how?

For step-by-step practice in the writing process, see the *Writing Activity Book, High Intermediate,* Unit 1.

Assignment	Opinion paragraph
Prewriting	Group brainstorming
Organizing	Meeting the reader's expectations
Revising	Writing topic and concluding sentences
	Choosing active or passive voice
Editing	Using capitalization

For Unit 1 Internet activities, visit the NorthStar Companion Website at http://www.longman.com/northstar

Dreams Never Die

1 Focus on the Topic

A PREDICTING

Look at the photograph of Helen Keller and the title of the unit. Read the quotation below. Then discuss these questions with a partner.

"Although the world is full of suffering, it is also full of overcoming it."

—Helen Keller

1. There are many different types of suffering: physical and economic are two examples. What are some other examples of ways that people suffer?

2. What are some ways that people overcome their suffering?

3. What do you think the title of the unit means? What do you think this unit will be about?

B   SHARING INFORMATION

1 *Match the person with the obstacle he or she has overcome. Then answer the questions that follow with a partner.*

a. *Anne Frank*

b. *Tom Cruise*

c. *Walt Disney*

d. *Amelia Earhart*

_____ **1.** At age 22, this person was so poor that he "slept on cushions from an old sofa and ate cold beans out of a can." He was also fired by a newspaper editor for having no imagination.

_____ **2.** This person became the first woman to fly across the Atlantic. She faced two obstacles: prejudice and lack of money.

_____ **3.** This person spent 25 months hiding from the Nazis in an attic with her family during World War II. The diary she wrote while hiding has become one of the most widely read books in the world.

_____ **4.** This person has a reading problem called dyslexia. He learns his movie scripts by listening to tapes, not by reading them.

2 *There are many different types of obstacles. For example, being deaf is a physical obstacle. What type of obstacle did each of the people above overcome?*

3 *Can you think of any other famous people who have overcome obstacles?*

4 *What obstacles have you overcome in your life?*

C   PREPARING TO READ

BACKGROUND

Frank McCourt was born in Brooklyn, New York, in 1930. His parents, Angela and Malachy, had moved to New York from Ireland in search of a better life. Unfortunately, life was not easy in New York. His father could not earn enough money to support his family. The McCourts returned to Ireland hoping their life would improve. Again, it didn't. Life in Ireland was equally hard if not harder than in New York. Three of Frank's siblings died as babies. Eventually, his father <u>abandoned</u> the family, forcing his four sons and Angela to live a very <u>meager</u> existence.

Frank's childhood was filled with <u>misery</u>. There was never enough food. Their house was small, dirty, and very cold in the wintertime. When it rained, the floor would flood with water. Frank and his brothers <u>yearned for</u> a better life.

Frank did, however, have ways to escape from his <u>tormented</u> childhood. He loved to read, and even though his <u>dilapidated</u> house had no electricity, he would read under the street lamp outside his home. He also had a strong sense of humor. Humor was the McCourts' defense against their life of relentless <u>poverty</u> and <u>hopelessness</u>. Even in the worst of times, the McCourts could find something to laugh about.

In 1949, Frank returned to the United States. He was a 19-year-old Irish boy with an eighth-grade education. He was full of <u>shame</u> about his past and often invented stories about his <u>sordid</u> childhood instead of telling the truth. However, Frank was never <u>defeated</u> by his obstacles; in fact, Frank eventually used his humor and his storytelling talents to overcome the challenges life had set before him.

Answer these questions with a partner.

1. Frank had a hard life growing up. What were some the obstacles or challenges he had to overcome?

2. What did Frank enjoy doing as a child?

3. Why did Frank reinvent his past when he came to America?

VOCABULARY FOR COMPREHENSION

Find the underlined words in the reading above. Write each word beside its synonym.

a. _____misery_____ sadness

b. _____ poor, sparse

c. _____ embarrassment

d. _____ beaten, overcome by

e. _____ desired, wanted

f. _____ painful

g. _____ immoral, dishonest

h. _____ having little money or few material things

i. _____ left

j. _____ being without hope

k. _____ falling apart, in terrible condition

2 Focus on Reading

Read the first two paragraphs and answer the following questions with a partner. Then read the rest of the article.

1. Where is Frank McCourt now?

2. What do you think he means by *"They gave me so much more than I gave them?"*

3. What do you think happened to Frank between 1979 and 1997?

The Education of Frank McCourt

By Barbara Sande Dimmitt (from *Reader's Digest*)

1   Frank McCourt sat on a stage in New York City's Lincoln Center, his white hair glistening under the lights overhead. He was still boyish of expression at 66, and smile lines radiated from hazel eyes bright with inquisitiveness. Soon he would be addressing the 1997 graduating class of Stuyvesant High School, where he had taught English for 18 years.

2   He let his mind wander as he gazed out at the great hall. *I've learned so much from kids like these,* he thought. *They gave me much more than I gave them.*

3   "Yo, Teach!" a voice boomed. Frank McCourt scanned the adolescents in his classroom. It was the fall of 1970 and his first week of teaching at Seward Park High School, which sat in the midst of dilapidated tenement buildings on Manhattan's Lower East Side. McCourt located the speaker and nodded. "You talk funny," the student said. "Where ya from?"

4   "Ireland," McCourt replied. With more than ten years of teaching experience under his belt, this kind of interrogation[1] no longer surprised him. But one question in particular still made him squirm:[2] "Where'd you go to high school?" someone else asked.

5   If I tell them the truth, they'll feel superior to me, McCourt thought. They'll throw it in

---

[1] *interrogation:* intense questioning
[2] *squirm:* feel embarrassed

my face. Most of all, he feared an accusation he'd heard before—from himself: You come from nothing, so you are nothing.

6   But McCourt's heart whispered another possibility: maybe these kids are yearning for a way of figuring out this new teacher. Am I willing to risk being humiliated in the classroom to find out?

7   "Come on, tell us! Where'd you go to high school?"

8   "I never did," McCourt replied.

9   "Did you get thrown out?"

10   I was right, the teacher thought. They're curious. McCourt explained he'd left school after the eighth grade to take a job.

11   "How'd you get to be a teacher, then?" they asked. "When I came to America," he began, "I dreamed bigger dreams. I loved reading and writing, and teaching was the most exalted profession I could imagine. I was unloading sides of beef³ down on the docks when I decided enough was enough. By then I'd done a lot of reading on my own, so I persuaded New York University to enroll me."

12   McCourt wasn't surprised that this story fascinated his students. Theirs wasn't the kind of poverty McCourt had known; they had electricity and food. But he recognized the telltale signs of need in some of his students' threadbare⁴ clothes, and sensed the bitter shame and hopelessness he knew all too well. If recounting his own experiences would jolt these kids out of their defeatism so he could teach them something, that's what he would do.

13   A born storyteller, McCourt drew from a repertoire of accounts about his youth. His students would listen, spellbound⁵ by the gritty details, drawn by something more powerful than curiosity. He'd look from face to face, recognizing a bit of himself in each sober gaze.

14   Since humor had been the McCourts' weapon against life's miseries in Limerick, he used it to describe those days. "Dinner usually was bread and tea," he told the students. "Mam⁶ used to say, 'We've got our balanced diet: a solid and a liquid. What more could we want?'"

15   The students roared with laughter.

16   He realized that his honesty was helping forge a link with kids who normally regarded teachers as adversaries. At the same time, the more he talked about his past, the better he understood how it affected him.

17   [While at college], a creative-writing professor had asked him to describe an object from his childhood. McCourt chose the decrepit bed he and his brothers had shared. He wrote of their being scratched by the stiff stuffing protruding from the mattress and of ending up jumbled together in the sagging center with fleas⁷ leaping all over their bodies. The professor gave McCourt an A, and asked him to read the essay to the class.

18   "No!" McCourt said, recoiling at the thought. But for the first time, he began to see his sordid childhood, with all the miseries, betrayals and longings that tormented him still, as a worthy topic. Maybe that's what I was born to put on the page,⁸ he thought.

19   While teaching, McCourt wrote occasional articles for newspapers and magazines. But his major effort, a memoir of 150 pages that he churned out in 1966, remained unfinished. Now he leafed through his students' transcribed essays. They lacked polish, but somehow they worked in a way his writing didn't. I'm trying to teach these kids to write, he thought, yet I haven't found the secret myself.

³ *sides of beef:* meat
⁴ *threadbare:* very worn
⁵ *spellbound:* very interested
⁶ *Mam:* a word for *mother*
⁷ *fleas:* tiny insects
⁸ *put on the page:* to write

20   The bell rang in the faculty lounge at Stuyvesant High School in Manhattan. When McCourt began teaching at the prestigious[9] public high school in 1972, he joked that he'd finally made it to paradise. Some 13,000 students sought admission each year, competing for approximately 700 vacancies. Part of the fun of working with these bright students was keeping them a few degrees off-balance. McCourt asked at the beginning of a creative-writing class, "What did you have for dinner last night?" The students stared at him as if he'd lost his wits.

21   "Why am I asking this? Because you need to become good observers of detail if you're going to write well." As answers trickled in, McCourt countered with more questions. "Where did you eat?" "Who else was there?" "Who cleaned up afterward?"

22   Student after student revealed families fragmented by divorce and loneliness. "We always argue at the table." "We don't eat together." As he listened, McCourt mentally catalogued the differences and similarities between his early life and theirs. He began to appreciate more the companionship that enriched the meager meals his mother had struggled to put on the table.

23   That night McCourt lay awake in bed, harvesting the bounty of his chronic insomnia. He visualized himself standing on a street in Limerick, and took an imaginary walk about. He looked at shops and pubs, noting their names, and peered through their windows. He read street signs and recognized people walking past. Oblivious to time, he wandered the Limerick of his mind, collecting the details of scenery and a cast for the book that festered inside him.

24   Yet when he later picked up a notebook and tried to set down the previous night's travels, he stopped. McCourt knew that he was still holding back. Before, he had done

it out of respect for his mother, who would have been mortified to see the darkest and most searing episodes of his childhood in print.[10] But she had died in 1981, and with her had died his excuse.

25   At least the bits and pieces that bubbled into his consciousness enlivened the stories he told in class. "Everyone has a story to tell," he said. "Write about what you know with conviction, from the heart. Dig deep," he urged. "Find your own voice and dance your own dance!"

26   On Fridays the students read their compositions aloud. To draw them out, McCourt would read excerpts from his duffel bag full of notebooks. "You had such an interesting childhood, Mr. McCourt," they said. "Why don't you write a book?" They threw his own words back at him: "It sounds like there's more to that story; dig deeper. . ."

27   McCourt was past 50 and painfully aware of the passage of time. But despite his growing frustration at his unfinished book, he never tired of his students' work.

28   These young people have been giving you lessons in courage, he thought. When will you dare as mightily as they?

29   It was October 1994. Frank McCourt, now retired, sat down and read his book's new opening, which he had written a few days before and still found satisfying. But many blank pages lay before him. What if I never get it right? he wondered grimly.

30   He stared at the logs glowing in the fireplace and could almost hear students' voices from years past, some angry, some defeated, others confused and seeking guidance. "It's no good, Mr. McCourt. I don't have what it takes."

31   Then Frank McCourt, author, heard the steadying tones of Frank McCourt, teacher: Of course you do. Dig deeper. Find your own voice and dance your own dance.

[9] *prestigious:* of high status
[10] *in print:* in a book, newspaper, magazine

32   He scribbled a few lines. "I'm in a playground on Classon Avenue in Brooklyn with my brother Malachy. He's two, I'm three. We're on the seesaw." In the innocent voice of an unprotected child who could neither comprehend nor control the world around him, Frank McCourt told his tale of poverty and abandonment.

33   In September 1996 *Angela's Ashes* hit bookstores. Within weeks McCourt received an excited call from his agent: his book was getting warm reviews and selling at an unbelievable rate. The most surprising call came on April 7, 1997, when McCourt learned that *Angela's Ashes* had received America's most coveted literary award: the Pulitzer Prize.

34   McCourt laid his hands on the lectern, finishing his commencement address[11] at Lincoln Center. "Early in my teaching days, the kids asked me the meaning of a poem," he said. "I replied, 'I don't know any more than you do. I have ideas. What are your ideas?' I realized then that we're all in the same boat. What does anybody know?

35   "So when you go forth tonight, fellow students—for I'm still one of you—remember that you know nothing! Be excited that your whole life is before you for learning."

36   As he gave them a crooked smile, the students leapt to their feet, waving and whistling. This is too much, he thought, startled by the intensity of their response. During months of speeches and book signings, he had received many accolades[12]. But this—this left him fighting back tears. It's the culmination of everything, coming from them.

37   Their standing ovation continued long after Frank McCourt, the teacher who had learned his own lessons slowly but well, returned to his seat.

---

[11] *commencement address:* speech given at a graduation
[12] *accolades:* high praise

READING FOR MAIN IDEAS

Complete the time line with information from Preparing to Read on pages 24–25 and Reading One.

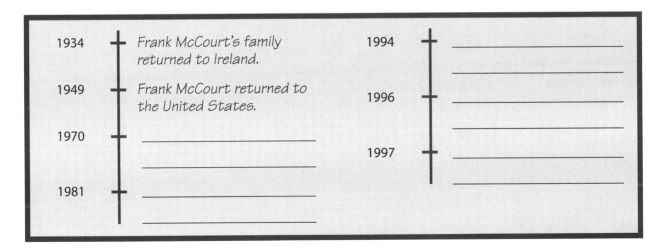

1934	Frank McCourt's family returned to Ireland.
1949	Frank McCourt returned to the United States.
1970	_____
1981	_____

1994	_____
1996	_____
1997	_____

READING FOR DETAILS

Complete the left side of the chart using information from Reading for Main Ideas on page 29. Then complete the right side of the chart with details about why the event took place and what happened as a result. Look back at Preparing to Read on pages 24–25 and Reading One for the information.

1934 **Event:** *Frank McCourt's family returned to Ireland.*	*The McCourts wanted a better life, so they returned to Ireland. Their life was still very hard. Three children died. The family remained very poor and very hungry.*
1949 **Event:**	
1970 **Event:**	
1981 **Event:**	
1994 **Event:**	
1996 **Event:**	
1997 **Event:**	

REACTING TO THE READING

1 *Read the following excerpts from the reading. Choose the interpretation that best explains the meaning of the underlined sentences.*

1. Most of all, he feared an accusation he'd heard before—from himself: <u>You come from nothing, so you are nothing</u>.
   a. People who have nothing have no value.
   b. Only people who come from "good families" can make something of themselves.
   c. People from poor countries have no value.

2. His students would listen, spellbound by the gritty details, drawn by something more powerful than curiosity. <u>He'd look from face to face, recognizing a bit of himself in each sober gaze.</u>
   a. McCourt's students reminded him of what he was like at that age.
   b. McCourt's students looked a lot like he looked at that age.
   c. McCourt's students recognized him as their teacher.

3. He realized that his honesty was helping forge a link with kids who normally regarded teachers as adversaries. <u>At the same time, the more he talked about his past, the better he understood how it affected him.</u>
   a. His past affected him when he talked about it.
   b. Because he understood that his past affected him, he talked a lot about it.
   c. Talking about his past helped him to realize its importance in his life.

4. "Write about what you know with conviction, from the heart. <u>Dig deep," he urged. "Find your own voice and dance your own dance!"</u>
   a. Try hard! You must talk loudly so everyone hears you.
   b. Try hard! You must write about what you know and in your own style. Don't copy others.
   c. Try hard! Sing and dance through life!

5. These young people have been giving you lessons in courage, he thought. <u>When will you dare as mightily as they?</u>
   a. When will you take the chances they have (in your writing?)
   b. When will you challenge them in their writing?
   c. When will they challenge you?

2 *Discuss these questions with a partner.*

1. What do you think was Frank McCourt's greatest obstacle? How did he overcome it?

2. How did Frank McCourt's students give him the courage he had been lacking to overcome his obstacles?

B READING TWO: *The Miracle*

Diane Schuur is an accomplished jazz musician who is blind. In the following reading, she compares her struggles and triumphs with those of Helen Keller, a famous writer and political activist who was not only blind, but deaf as well.

Discuss these questions with a partner.

1. What do you think "She altered our perception of the disabled and remapped the boundaries of sight and sense" means?

2. How do you think Diane Schuur "remapped" her boundaries?

Diane Schuur

The Miracle: *She altered our perception of the disabled and remapped the boundaries of sight and sense.*

By Diane Schuur (from *Time*)

1   Helen Keller was less than two years old when she came down with a fever. It struck dramatically and left her unconscious. The fever went just as suddenly. But she was blinded and, very soon after, deaf. As she grew up, she managed to learn to do tiny errands, but she also realized that she was missing something. "Sometimes," she later wrote, "I stood between two persons who were conversing and touched their lips. I could not understand, and was vexed. I moved my lips and gesticulated frantically without result. This made me so angry at times that I kicked and screamed until I was exhausted." She was a wild child.

2   I can understand her rage. I was born two months prematurely and was placed in an incubator. The practice at the time was to pump a large amount of oxygen into the incubator, something doctors have since learned to be extremely cautious about. But as a result, I lost my sight. I was sent to a state school for the blind, but I flunked first grade because Braille[1] just didn't make any sense to me. Words were a weird concept. I remember being hit and slapped. And you act all that in. All rage is anger that is acted in, bottled in for so long that it just pops out. Helen had it harder. She was both blind and deaf. But, oh, the transformation that came over her when she discovered that words were related to things! It's like the lyrics of that song: "On a clear day, rise and look around you, and you'll see who you are."

[1] *Braille:* a form of printing with raised round marks that blind people can read by touching

3   I can say the word see. I can speak the language of the sighted. That's part of the first great achievement of Helen Keller. She proved how language could liberate the blind and the deaf. She wrote, "Literature is my utopia. Here I am not disenfranchised." But how she struggled to master language. In her book *Midstream,* she wrote about how she was frustrated by the alphabet, by the language of the deaf, even with the speed with which her teacher spelled things out for her on her palm. She was impatient and hungry for words, and her teacher's scribbling on her hand would never be as fast, she thought, as the people who could read the words with their eyes. I remember how books got me going after I finally grasped Braille. Being in that school was like being in an orphanage. But words—and in my case, music—changed that isolation. With language, Keller, who could not hear and could not see, proved she could communicate in the world of sight and sound—and was able to speak to it and live in it. I am a beneficiary of her work. Because of her example, the world has given way a little. In my case, I was able to go from the state school for the blind to regular public school from the age of 11 until my senior year in high school. And then I decided on my own to go back into the school for the blind. Now I sing jazz.

4   I hate the word handicapped. Keller would too. We are people with inconveniences. We're not charity cases. Her main message was and is, "We're like everybody else. We're here to be able to live a life as full as any sighted person's. And it's O.K. to be ourselves."

5   That means we have the freedom to be as extraordinary as the sighted. Keller loved an audience and wrote that she adored "the warm tide of human life pulsing round and round me." That's why the stage appealed to her, why she learned to speak and to deliver speeches. And to feel the vibrations of music, of the radio, of the movement of lips. You must understand that even more than sighted people, we need to be touched. When you look at a person, eye to eye, I imagine it's like touching them. We don't have that convenience. But when I perform, I get that experience from a crowd. Helen Keller must have as well. She was our first star. And I am very grateful to her.

On a separate piece of paper, write short answers to the following questions. Discuss your answers with a partner.

1. How is Diane Schuur similar to Helen Keller? How is she different?

2. What does Diane Schuur mean by the following statements:

- "I hate the word handicapped. Keller would too. We are people with inconveniences. We're not charity cases."

- "You must understand that even more than sighted people, we need to be touched. When you look at a person, eye to eye, I imagine it's like touching them. We don't have that convenience. But when I perform, I get that experience from a crowd."

C   LINKING READINGS ONE AND TWO

1 *Both Frank McCourt and Diane Schuur faced many obstacles and challenges in their lives. These same challenges also helped them to become talented and successful individuals. In this way, they are very similar. Complete the chart comparing Frank McCourt and Diane Schuur.*

	FRANK McCOURT	DIANE SCHUUR
Obstacles they faced		
People or person who influenced and inspired them		
Personal values, traits, or characteristics that helped them face their obstacles		
Talent or gift that resulted from the challenges they faced		

2 *Using the information in the chart above, write a short paragraph comparing the lives of Frank McCourt and Diane Schuur. Discuss their obstacles and triumphs.*

3 Focus on Vocabulary

1 *The diagram on page 35 depicts three stages of overcoming obstacles: facing the obstacle, dealing with the obstacle, and overcoming the obstacle. Read the words in the box and decide which stages they describe. Write the words in the appropriate circle.*

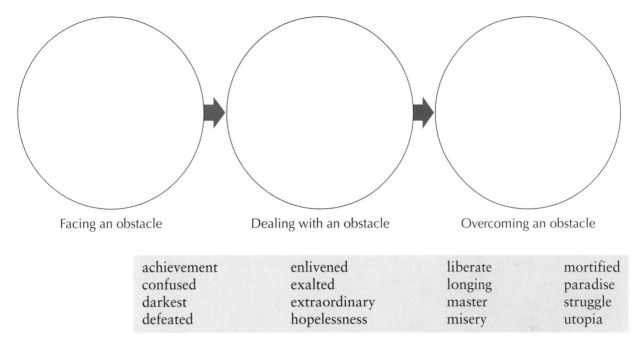

Facing an obstacle   Dealing with an obstacle   Overcoming an obstacle

achievement	enlivened	liberate	mortified
confused	exalted	longing	paradise
darkest	extraordinary	master	struggle
defeated	hopelessness	misery	utopia

2 *Work with a partner. Read the following sentences and circle the letter of the best explanation.*

1. If I tell them the truth, they'll feel superior to me, McCourt thought. They'll throw it in my face.

   a. If I tell them the truth, they'll use it against me.

   b. If I tell them the truth, they'll refuse to look at me.

2. McCourt recognized the telltale signs of need in some of his students' threadbare clothes, and sensed the bitter shame and hopelessness he knew all too well.

   a. McCourt saw that the students were ashamed of their clothes and that they knew they would never get new ones.

   b. McCourt understood his students' poverty and humiliation because of his own past.

3. Since humor had been the McCourts' weapon against life's miseries in Limerick, he used it to describe those days.

   a. McCourt told of the problems of his life in Limerick using humor to overcome his sadness.

   b. McCourt reported about his comical life in Limerick.

4. McCourt realized that his honesty was helping forge a link with kids who normally regarded teachers as adversaries.

   a. Telling the truth about his past helped McCourt gain trust and friendship from his students, who normally did not trust teachers.

   b. McCourt's students were not friends with their teachers because they could not be honest with them.

5. McCourt began to see his sordid childhood, with all the miseries, betrayals and longings that tormented him still, as a worthy literary topic.
   a. Writing about his past was beginning to be a very painful process for McCourt.
   b. McCourt started to realize that all the problems of his childhood made good material for a book.

6. McCourt leafed through his students' essays. They lacked polish, but somehow they worked in a way his writing didn't.
   a. The essays were not perfectly written, but the content was interesting.
   b. The essays were perfectly written, but the content was not interesting.

7. Part of the fun of working with these bright students was keeping them a few degrees off balance.
   a. Working with intelligent students was not as much fun as McCourt thought.
   b. Making sure intelligent students were always surprised and interested made it fun to work with them.

8. McCourt's students stared at him as if he'd lost his wits.
   a. McCourt's students looked at him because he had no sense of humor.
   b. McCourt's students looked at him as if he were crazy.

9. After McCourt's students revealed, "We always argue at the table." "We don't eat together," he began to appreciate more the companionship that enriched the meager meals his mother had struggled to put on the table.
   a. Similar to his students, McCourt and his family always argued at the table because they didn't have a lot of food.
   b. After hearing his students' stories, McCourt realized that although his family didn't have much food, at least they ate together and enjoyed each other's company.

10. That night McCourt lay awake in bed, harvesting the bounty of his chronic insomnia. He visualized himself standing on a street in Limerick, and took an imaginary walk about.
    a. That night McCourt couldn't sleep so he got up and walked around Limerick.
    b. When McCourt couldn't sleep that night, he thought in great detail about his past.

11. McCourt said, "I don't know any more than you do. I have ideas. What are your ideas?" He realized then that they were all in the same boat. What does anybody know?
    a. He realized that he and his students were all equal.
    b. He realized that he and his students all came from the same country.

3 *Choose one of the following situations and write a letter. In your letter, use words and phrases from Exercises 1 and 2.*

    1. Imagine you are Diane Schuur. Write a letter to Helen Keller. Explain how she helped you and inspired you to overcome your obstacles.

    2. Imagine you are one of Frank McCourt's former students. You have just graduated from college. Write a letter to Frank McCourt. Explain how he helped and inspired you to overcome an obstacle.

4 Focus on Writing

A GRAMMAR: Gerunds and Infinitives

1 *Examine the following sentences and answer the questions with a partner.*

    a. <u>Teaching</u> was the most exalted profession I could imagine.

    b. McCourt enjoyed <u>reading</u> and <u>writing</u>.

    c. McCourt had done a lot of <u>reading</u>.

    d. Helen Keller learned <u>to deliver</u> speeches.

    e. I persuaded New York University <u>to enroll</u> me.

    f. After McCourt's mother died, he felt free <u>to write</u> his memoirs.

    g. Helen Keller said the blind have the freedom <u>to be</u> as extraordinary as the sighted.

1. In sentence *a*, what is the subject?

2. In sentence *b*, what is the object of the verb?

3. In sentence *c*, what word follows the preposition *of*?

4. Look at the underlined words in *a*, *b*, and *c*. They are gerunds. How are gerunds formed?

5. In sentence *d*, the main verb is *learned*. What is the verb that follows it?

6. In sentence *e*, the main verb is *persuaded*. What is the object of the main verb? What is the verb that follows it?

7. In sentence *f*, what is the verb that follows the adjective *free*?

8. In sentence *g*, what is the verb that follows the noun *freedom*?

9. Look at the underlined words in *d*, *e*, *f*, and *g*. They are infinitives. How are infinitives formed?

Gerunds and Infinitives

Gerunds

To form a gerund, add **-ing** to the base form of the verb.

Use the gerund:

1. as the subject of a sentence

Writing is very important to Frank McCourt.

2. as the object of a sentence after certain verbs (such as *enjoy, acknowledge, recall*)

Frank McCourt enjoys **writing**.

3. after a preposition (such as *of, in, for, about*)

Frank McCourt is interested in **writing**.

Infinitives

To form an infinitive, use **to** and the base form of the verb.

Use the infinitive:

4. after certain verbs

  a. some verbs are followed directly by an infinitive (such as *learn, decide, agree*)

McCourt's students **learned to write** about their personal experiences.

  b. some verbs are followed by an object + an infinitive (such as *urge, persuade*)

McCourt **urged his students to write** about their personal experiences.

  c. some verbs are followed by an infinitive or an object + an infinitive (such as *want, ask, need*)

McCourt **wanted to write** about personal experiences.
McCourt **wanted them to write** about their personal experiences.

5. after certain adjectives (such as *free, able, hard*)

McCourt's students were free **to write** about whatever they wanted.

6. after certain nouns (such as *ability, freedom*)

McCourt's students had the freedom **to write** about whatever they wanted.

2 *Work with a partner. Underline the gerund or infinitive in the following sentences. Which rule in the grammar box on page 38 applies to each sentence? Write the number of the rule in the space next to each sentence.*

__1__ **a.** <u>Learning</u> Braille was difficult for Diane Schuur.

_____ **b.** McCourt had the ability to describe objects from his childhood.

_____ **c.** McCourt acknowledged not going to high school.

_____ **d.** Helen Keller was able to live in the world of sight and sound.

_____ **e.** A professor asked McCourt to describe an object from his childhood.

_____ **f.** Diane Schuur decided to go back into the school for the blind.

_____ **g.** Many people don't feel free to write about their lives.

_____ **h.** Recounting his experiences inspired McCourt's students.

_____ **i.** McCourt couldn't think about writing his memoirs while his mother was alive.

_____ **j.** Diane Schuur wants people to think of her as inconvenienced, not handicapped.

3 *Read the following information about Frank McCourt, Diane Schuur, and Helen Keller. Rewrite each situation using a form of the first verb given and the gerund or infinitive form of the second verb.*

1. McCourt was worried his memoirs would embarrass his mother. After she died, he didn't have to worry about this.

   After his mother died, McCourt felt free to write his memoirs.
   (feel free/write)

2. As a child, Helen Keller was impatient and hungry for words. She was frustrated because she couldn't talk to people.

   _____
   (want/communicate)

3. McCourt had no high school education, but he had read a lot. He told New York University it should admit him.

   _____
   (persuade/allow)

4. Diane Schuur sings and plays jazz. She likes the feeling she gets from a crowd.

   _____
   (enjoy/perform)

5. Frank McCourt hadn't gone to high school. He was afraid of what his students would think about him.

   _____
   (worry about/tell)

6. Diane Schuur first went to a school for the blind and after that to regular public school from age 11 until she was a senior in high school. Then she thought she should go back to the school for the blind.

_____
(decide/return)

7. McCourt's students didn't think they were able to write. He gave them lots of encouragement and told them "everyone has a story to tell."

_____
(urge/write)

8. Helen Keller was blind and deaf. She struggled with language.

_____
(be hard/learn)

9. McCourt remembered the town of Limerick. He could see and imagine what it was like when he was a child.

_____
(recall/live)

10. Diane Schuur could have gone to regular public school, or she could have gone to the state school for the blind.

_____
(be able/choose)

B STYLE: The Three-Part Paragraph

1 *Read this paragraph and discuss the questions with a partner.*

Helen Keller said, "Although the world is full of suffering, it is also full of overcoming it." This can be seen all around us. Many people have faced great obstacles in their lives but have found ways to overcome and actually benefit from these obstacles. For example, Greg Barton, the 1984, 1988, and 1992 U.S. Olympic medalist in kayaking, was born with a serious disability. He had club feet, his toes pointed inward, and as a result, he could not walk easily. Even after a series of operations, he still had limited mobility. Even so, Greg was never defeated. First, he taught himself to walk, and even to run. Then, he competed on his high school running team. He knew, though, he would never become an Olympic runner, so he looked for other sports that he could play. Happily, he discovered kayaking, a perfect sport for him because it required minimal leg and foot muscles. Using his upper body strength, he was able to master the sport. Finally, after many years of training and perseverance, Greg made the 1984 Olympic team. He says of his accomplishments, "Each step of the road has been made easier by looking just as far as necessary—yet not beyond that." In short, even though that road was paved with obstacles, he was able to overcome them and achieve the impossible.

1. What is the topic of the paragraph? How do you know?

2. What is the controlling idea?

3. What sentences support the topic and controlling ideas? How do they relate to the controlling idea?

4. What is the conclusion? How does it relate to the topic sentence?

NOTE: For more information on topic sentences and controlling ideas, see Unit 1.

The Three-Part Paragraph

A **paragraph** is a group of sentences that develops one main idea. There are usually three parts to a paragraph: the **topic sentence,** the **supporting sentences,** and the **concluding sentence.**

Topic Sentence

The topic sentence introduces the subject you are going to write about and your ideas or opinions about the subject. It controls what you write in the rest of the paragraph. For example, in the paragraph on page 40, the first sentence is the topic sentence. It introduces the topic (suffering) and the controlling idea (overcoming suffering). All the sentences in the paragraph must relate to, describe, or exemplify the topic sentence.

Supporting Sentences

The second part of the paragraph includes sentences that give details or examples that develop your ideas about the topic. This part of the paragraph is usually the longest, since it discusses and explains the controlling idea. In the paragraph on page 40, the sentences give examples of how Greg did not give in to his problems but instead tried to overcome them by forcing himself to run, and then working hard to become an Olympic champion.

Concluding Sentence

The last part of the paragraph can do one or more of the following. It can summarize the paragraph, offer a solution to the problem, restate the introductory sentence, or offer an opinion. The paragraph on page 40 concludes with: "In short, even though that road was paved with obstacles, he was able to overcome them and achieve the impossible." Here, the concluding sentence restates the ideas in the topic sentence, "Although the world is full of suffering, it is also full of overcoming it."

(continued)

Transitions

Transitions are words and phrases that signal connections among ideas. They are often used to begin supporting sentences and concluding sentences to help the reader follow the progression of examples, details, and ideas. Some of these transitions are listed below.

Use	Transitions
first support	First, For one thing, First of all
additional support	In addition, Furthermore, Moreover, Also, Another reason
examples	For example, For instance, Specifically
final support	Finally, Last of all
conclusion	In short, In conclusion, In summary

NOTE: Transitions are generally followed by a comma (,).

2 *Read each topic sentence. Two of the ideas that follow support the topic sentence and one does not. Cross out the idea that does not support the topic sentence.*

1. Ever since Greg Barton was in high school, he longed to be an Olympic champion.
   a. Greg's sports records
   b. How Greg trained for the Olympics
   c. ~~Greg's academic achievements~~

2. The achievements of people like Helen Keller and Diane Schuur have inspired many others.
   a. Explanation of how they have inspired others
   b. How many people have read about Helen Keller and Diane Schuur
   c. About Helen Keller's and Diane Schuur's obstacles

3. The poverty-stricken lives of Frank McCourt's students deeply affected him.
   a. How Frank saw himself in his students
   b. How Frank taught his students to write
   c. How the students inspired him to write

4. Learning to read Braille is a very difficult and frustrating process.
   a. The patience people need to learn Braille
   b. Reasons why people should learn Braille
   c. The amount of practice and time needed to learn Braille

3 *Each of the following paragraphs has one supporting sentence that does not directly relate to the topic sentence. Cross out the sentence and explain why it is unrelated.*

1. Helen Keller was very frustrated as a child. First of all, because she could neither hear nor speak, she couldn't understand what was happening around her. She felt her mother's lips moving as she spoke, but this made no sense to her. She couldn't understand what her mother was doing. ~~Her mother could hear and speak~~. Secondly, once she learned what words were, she felt she could never communicate with them as quickly as sighted people could. As a result of all of her frustration, she would often cry and scream until she was exhausted.

   Explanation: *The sentence focuses on her mother's abilities, not Helen's*
   frustrations.

2. The act of reading liberated Helen Keller, Diane Schuur, and Frank McCourt. All three of these people faced overwhelming obstacles, but literature freed them from their hardest struggles. For example, once Helen Keller and Diane Schuur learned to read Braille, a whole new world of books opened for them. In addition, Frank McCourt escaped his grim home life by reading as much as he could. They are all great writers and musicians.

   Explanation: _____
   _____

3. Some of the world's most talented and famous people have overcome some of the hardest obstacles. For example, Ludwig van Beethoven became deaf at age 46. Franklin D. Roosevelt was paralyzed by polio and was often in a wheelchair, but he was elected president of the United States four times. Finally, Steven Hawking is a world-famous scientist who is completely paralyzed. Furthermore, he lives in England. These people show us that we should never give up or let obstacles defeat us.

   Explanation: _____
   _____

4 *For each of the following topic sentences, write two or three supporting sentences. Use transitions.*

1. Facing your obstacles and overcoming them makes you a stronger person.

   _____

   _____

   _____

2. We should treat people with disabilities the same as we treat everyone else.

   _____

   _____

   _____

3. People who have overcome obstacles have some common characteristics.

   _____

   _____

   _____

4. You should face your obstacles and try to overcome them, not run away from them.

   _____

   _____

   _____

C WRITING TOPICS

Write a paragraph about one of these topics. Be sure to use some of the ideas, vocabulary, grammar, and style that you have learned in this unit.

1. Apply the following quote to a person you have read about from this unit, another famous person, or yourself. Write your response using examples.

   "When one door of happiness closes, another opens; but often we look so long at the closed door that we do not see the one which has been opened for us."
   —Helen Keller

2. Have you ever faced a great challenge or obstacle? What was it? Did it change your life? How? How did you overcome this obstacle and how did this experience affect you?

3. Think of a person you know personally who has overcome a great obstacle. What was the obstacle he or she faced? How did the person's life change because of the obstacle? What was his or her experience overcoming the obstacle and what effect did doing so have on his or her life?

4. What are two of the values and personal characteristics people need in order to overcome obstacles? How do people apply these values and characteristics to their lives?

D RESEARCH TOPIC

Many famous people have overcome great obstacles, including emotional, physical, and political obstacles. Research a person you admire or choose a person from the list below. Write a report, including answers to the following questions. Present your report to the class.

- What is (was) the person famous for?
- What did this person achieve?
- What obstacles did this person have to overcome? How did he or she overcome them?
- What personal characteristics helped this person overcome his or her obstacles?
- What has researching this person taught you about life and overcoming obstacles?

Artists / Performers
Christopher Reeve
Mary Cassat
Charlie Chaplin
Marc Chagall
Vincent Van Gogh
Michelangelo
Stevie Wonder

Sport Figures
Lance Armstrong
Jackie Robinson
Magic Johnson

Writers / Scientists
Steven Hawking
Sigmund Freud
Charles Darwin
Thomas Edison
Hans Christian Anderson

Politicians / Leaders
The Dalai Lama
Mahatma Ghandi
Golda Meir
Nelson Rockefeller

For step-by-step practice in the writing process, see the *Writing Activity Book, High Intermediate,* Unit 2.

Assignment	Biographical paragraph
Prewriting	Freewriting
Organizing	Planning a paragraph
Revising	Developing paragraph unity and coherence
	Using gerunds and infinitives
Editing	Using commas

For Unit 2 Internet activities, visit the NorthStar Companion Website at
http://www.longman.com/northstar

Dying for Their Beliefs

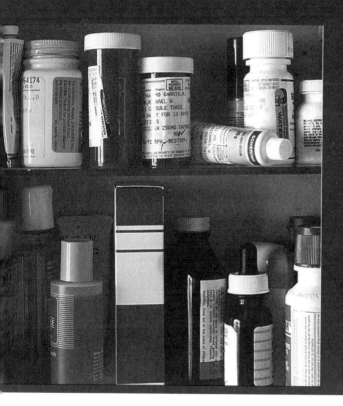

1 Focus on the Topic

A PREDICTING

Look at the photographs and the title of the unit. Then discuss these questions with a partner.

1. Which photograph shows conventional medical treatments and which shows nonconventional, or alternative, treatments?

2. Which of these treatments have you used? How do you decide which treatment to use and how much to use?

3. What do you think the title of the unit means? What do you think this unit will be about?

47

B   SHARING INFORMATION

Read the following statements regarding medicine. Write (A) if you agree or (D) if you disagree. Discuss your answers in small groups.

_____ 1. If you are sick, taking drugs (medicine) is the best way to get better.

_____ 2. Praying can cure sickness.

_____ 3. People who have a positive attitude will be cured faster than people with a negative attitude.

_____ 4. Medical treatments could be more effective if we also used alternative and natural or herbal remedies.

_____ 5. Patients have the right to choose the treatment they believe in, conventional or alternative, even if doctors do not agree.

_____ 6. Parents, rather than doctors or the government, have the right to choose the treatment they believe is best for their children.

C   PREPARING TO READ

BACKGROUND

Mary Baker Eddy was an American religious leader and the founder of the Christian Science movement. She was born in Bow, New Hampshire, in the United States, on July 16, 1821. As a child she was not very healthy and, as a result, she missed a great deal of school. Her education came through home schooling and study of the Bible and Scriptures.[1]

She continued to suffer from poor health as an adult and tried many alternative therapies including mesmerism (hypnosis), hydrotherapy (water cures), and mental healing. Once, after falling on ice and suffering a severe injury, she asked for her Bible and read a Gospel[2] account of one of Jesus's healings. After reading the New Testament,[3] she was completely cured and felt she had finally found the answer to her medical problems: the Scriptures.

Eddy believed that all sickness was mental rather than physical. She began the practice of healing others by reading the Bible and teaching others to be healers as well. In 1875, she published *Science and Health with Key to the Scriptures.* Eddy later published sixteen other books. In 1879, she founded the Church of Christ, Scientist, an organization she oversaw closely until her death.

---

[1] *Scriptures:* the writings of the Bible
[2] *Gospel:* from the Christian Bible, one of four stories of Christ's life
[3] *New Testament:* part of the Bible that is about Christ's life and his teachings

Her followers, called Christian Scientists, believe that disease, as well as sin and death, do not originate with God and, therefore, are not real. They see God as the only healer. Instead of medicinal remedies, Christian Scientists pray for the sick person. In addition, a church "practitioner"[4] prays for the sick and a church nurse gives nonmedical physical care.[5] The church, however, does not stop its members from seeing a doctor; it leaves the choice to the individual. The church does permit conventional treatment for "mechanical" problems such as broken bones and dental cavities.

Today there are over 2,700 Christian Science churches worldwide.

Not everyone believes in conventional medicine. Some people, including Mary Baker Eddy and her followers, do not agree that doctors, drugs, or surgery are the best ways to treat medical problems. Instead, they seek alternative types of medical care. What do you think about alternative medical care? Complete the following sentences and then discuss your answers with a partner.

1. Some people try nonconventional methods of healing because _____

   _____

   _____

2. Many people look to spiritual healing—reading religious scriptures and

   praying—to help them get better because _____

   _____

   _____

3. I agree / disagree with Mary Baker Eddy's philosophy that sickness originates

   in the mind because _____

   _____

   _____

---

[4] ***"practitioner":*** a person who has been schooled and trained in praying for the sick
[5] ***nonmedical physical care:*** care that includes taking care of hygiene and dietary needs as well as caring for wounds and injuries; does not include giving any medication.

VOCABULARY FOR COMPREHENSION

Reading One examines the role of the legal system in controlling a person's choice of medical treatment. Look at the list of words and write each word in the correct category below. Discuss the meaning of the words with a partner. Note that some words may belong to both categories. If you need help, use a dictionary.

Verb Phrases
commit a crime
convict
heal
shed weight
stand trial
suffer

Nouns
accuser   felony
ailment   manslaughter
attorney   physician
autopsy   practitioner
diabetes   prosecutor

LEGAL SYSTEM VOCABULARY	MEDICAL VOCABULARY

2 Focus on Reading

A   READING ONE: *Dying for Their Beliefs*

Read the first three paragraphs. Work with a partner to answer the questions. Then read the rest of the article.

1. What is the problem?

2. What do you think is happening to Amy?

Dying for Their Beliefs: Christian Scientist Parents on Trial in Girl's Death

By Jeffrey Good (from the *St. Petersburg Times*)

1   Amy Hermanson was a sunny seven-year-old with blond hair and bubbly ways. She liked to serenade adults with her favorite song: Disney's "It's a Small World After All."

2   But Amy's world went awry[1] one Sunday in 1986. An adult friend of her family noticed the child's sunken eyes, her listless[2] manner, the way her clothes hung from her tiny bones. She tried to get the child to sing her favorite song.

3   "She used to come over and sing every verse to me. I couldn't even get her to make a comment on the song, let alone sing it," the friend, Mary Christman, would later tell investigators. She recalled her husband saying, "If the child does not receive medical attention, she will be dead within a week."

4   But Amy's parents are Christian Scientists. They decided to try to heal the child with prayer rather than seek a doctor's aid. Two days after the Christmans saw her, Amy died of diabetes.

5   On Monday, Amy's parents are scheduled to go on trial in the Sarasota County Courthouse on charges of third-degree murder[3] and felony child abuse.[4] Prosecutors say William and Christine Hermanson committed a crime by putting religious principles ahead of protecting their daughter. The Hermansons say their accusers are wrong. If

convicted, the couple could face three to seven years in jail.

6   At issue is a legal principle with national ramifications. Since 1967, no Christian Scientist in the United States has stood trial for denying children medical care for religious reasons. Six similar cases are pending, but the Hermansons are the first to go to court.

7   "The children are entitled to protection, and if the parents won't give it to them, they [the parents] will suffer the [legal] consequences," says Mack Futch, an assistant state attorney in Sarasota County.

8   The Hermansons, however, have maintained that prosecutors want to violate their constitutional right of religious freedom. And in interviews last week, their supporters maintained that the couple treated their daughter with a proven—if unconventional—method of healing.

9   Frederick Hillier, a Christian Science "practitioner" who was ministering to the child when she died, said that Christian Scientists regard prayer as a better treatment than conventional medicine. "A Christian Scientist is doing nothing any different than

---

[1] *awry:* wrong, to not happen as planned
[2] *listless:* lacking energy
[3] *third-degree murder:* murder without intention
[4] *felony child abuse:* a serious crime involving hurting a child physically or psychologically

anyone who has found medical treatment to be effective," said Hillier, who also acts as the spokesman for Florida Christian Science churches. "Why do Christian Scientists rely on spiritual healing when they could go to a physician if they wanted to? In their experience, they found it to be effective."

10   Church members acknowledge that their methods sometimes fail, just as doctors sometimes fail, he said. But that doesn't mean the Christian Scientists deserve criminal charges any more than the doctors do, he said. "We don't claim any more than anyone else claims to be 100 percent effective," Hillier said. "Even Jesus didn't."

11   Amy's third grade report card was her last. It showed A's in reading, English, spelling, mathematics, science, and social studies. "Amy takes a keen interest in all her work," a teacher wrote.

12   But in September 1986, Amy began fourth grade as a different child. Teachers noticed her dozing off in class, shedding weight at an alarming rate, and complaining of stomachaches. At one point, she held her hands over her ears and pleaded, "Stop the noise. Stop the noise," at the sound of a pencil scratching paper.

13   "After the school year began, Amy was often upset. She would cry and say that she did not feel well," said June R. McHugh, director of the private Julie Rohr Academy attended by Amy and her older brother, Eric. McHugh told investigators that about a week before Amy's death, she told Mrs. Hermanson her daughter might be suffering from a physical ailment. McHugh recalled that Mrs. Hermanson said, "the situation was being handled."

14   On September 22, one of the practitioners began praying for the child.

15   On September 25, the Hermansons left Amy in a baby-sitter's care and went to Indiana for a Christian Science conference on spiritual healing. They returned on September 29.

16   But at 8:30 A.M. on September 30, 1986, a state social worker in Sarasota took a call from Amy's aunt. The worker's notes sketched a chilling picture: "Over the last two weeks (Amy) has lost 10 pounds, drinks constantly, eats large amounts of food, muscle tone is virtually gone, eyes are sunken and functioning separately. Child can barely walk and has to be carried—All indications point to diabetes but parents refuse to take said child to the doctor as they are Christian Scientists."

17   A court hearing was scheduled for 1:30 P.M. and Amy's father arrived early. At 1:27 P.M., Hermanson took a phone call from home reporting that Amy had taken a turn for the worse and an ambulance was en route. Learning this, the judge ordered that a medical doctor examine Amy.

18   But it was too late. With Christian Science practitioner Hillier nearby, Amy had died in her parents' bed.

Most Important Right

19   After performing an autopsy on the child, Associate Medical Examiner James C. Wilson concluded that medical treatment up to just hours before her death probably could have saved Amy. The Hermansons have acknowledged they never sought such treatment. That does not make them criminals, say their lawyers and supporters.

20   "There isn't anyone who is more loving to their children than Christian Scientists," said Bob Drabik, chairman of the board of directors at Sarasota's First Church, Christian Science, where the Hermansons are members.

21   Florida law says parents can't be judged "abusive or neglectful" because they withhold conventional medical treatment for religious reasons. Similar laws exist in most states. They were enacted under heavy lobbying from the Boston-based church after one of its members, Dorothy Sheridan of Harwich, Massachusetts, was convicted in

1967 of manslaughter in the death of her child. "William and Christine Hermanson, at all times material[5] to the facts in this case, followed the religious teachings of their church and relied upon Christian Science healing in the care and treatment of Amy Hermanson," the court record states.

22   Within the legal community, there is considerable debate over whether that is an adequate defense when a child dies. Harvard law professor Alan Dershowitz says that such trials revolve around two important constitutional rights: parents' freedom of religion, and children's right to grow up healthy.

23   In cases where one right must take priority, Dershowitz says, the choice is clear: "It's not a difficult question. Children have a right to live and be brought up to make their own religious decisions."

24   Hillier, the Christian Science spokesman, said that church members view prayer as the best way to make sick children well. "We don't want the right to do harm to children," he said, "we only want the right to do what is good for children."

[5] *material:* important to, related to

READING FOR MAIN IDEAS

Complete the following sentences based on your understanding of the reading. Compare sentences with a partner.

1. Amy's disease was _____

_____

2. Amy might have been saved if _____

_____

3. Her parents are going on trial because _____

_____

4. Christian Scientists and other supporters defend the Hermansons because ___

_____

5. Some people in the legal community believe that the two main issues are:

    a. _____

    b. _____

READING FOR DETAILS

*Write true (**T**) or false (**F**) for each sentence.*

_____ 1. If Amy had received medical care just two hours before she died, she probably could have been saved.

_____ 2. Some of the symptoms of Amy's disease were: loss of weight, stomachaches, and an intense interest in schoolwork.

_____ 3. The Hermansons feel children have the right to make their own religious decisions.

_____ 4. Christian Scientists and their supporters believe they want only to do what is good for their children.

_____ 5. Christian Scientists believe prayer is better than conventional medicine.

_____ 6. In Florida, parents can be judged "abusive or neglectful" if they choose to deny their children conventional medical care for religious reasons.

REACTING TO THE READING

1 *Work in a group. Decide which person could have made each statement. Write the correct letter in the space next to each statement. In some cases, more than one person could have made the statement. Refer to the reading to support your answers.*

a. Amy Hermanson, sick child

b. Alan Dershowitz, Harvard law professor

c. Mack Futch, assistant state attorney

d. Frederick Hillier, Christian Science "practitioner" and spokesman

e. Dorothy Sheridan, Christian Scientist convicted of manslaughter

f. James C. Wilson, associate medical examiner

_____ 1. If parents don't give their children medical protection, then the court system or the government must get involved.

_____ 2. Prayer, although not always effective, is the best treatment available.

_____ 3. The Hermansons are responsible for Amy's death.

_____ 4. This was a senseless death. Medically, it could have been prevented.

_____ 5. Our right to religious freedom allows us to decide what is best for our children.

_____ 6. Being a good student is easy if you can concentrate on your schoolwork.

_____ 7. Children should be able to live long enough to make their own religious decisions.

_____ 8. It's worth being convicted of a crime if what we do is for the benefit of our children.

_____ 9. Spiritual healing is just as legitimate a type of medical treatment as drugs.

_____ 10. A child's right to live is more important than his or her parents' religious beliefs.

2 *Discuss these questions in small groups. Then share your ideas with the class.*

1. Do you think Amy's parents are responsible for her death? Why or why not? If so, what punishment do you think they should receive?

2. Look back at your answers to Sharing Information on page 48. After reading about Amy, would you still answer these questions the same way? If not, how and why would your answers change?

3. Alan Dershowitz says that such trials revolve around two important constitutional rights: parents' freedom of religion and children's right to grow up healthy. What does he mean by this? How does it apply to Amy's situation?

B   READING TWO: *Norman Cousins's Laugh Therapy*

Norman Cousins was a well-known American writer and editor. When he was diagnosed with a serious illness, he decided to find his own type of alternative therapy. He focused on the importance of a positive attitude in healing. After writing about his successful recovery, he received mail from all over the world. Many letters came from doctors who supported his ideas.

Norman Cousins lived for 26 years after he became ill. He died in 1990 at the age of 75.

Charlie Chaplin, comedian

Discuss these questions with a partner.

1. What do you think Norman Cousins meant by "a positive attitude in healing"?

2. What do you think you can do to have a positive attitude?

3. Look at the photograph of Charlie Chaplin. Why do you think he could be associated with a positive attitude in healing?

Norman Cousins's Laugh Therapy

1   In the summer of 1964, well-known writer and editor Norman Cousins became very ill. His body ached and he felt constantly tired. It was difficult for him to even move around. He consulted his physician, who did many tests. Eventually he was diagnosed as having ankylosing spondylitis, a very serious and destructive form of arthritis.[1] His doctor told him that he would become immobilized[2] and eventually die from the disease. He was told he had only a 1 in 500 chance of survival.

2   Despite the diagnosis,[3] Cousins was determined to overcome the disease and survive. He had always been interested in medicine and had read the work of organic chemist Hans Selye, *The Stress of Life* (1956). This book discussed the idea of how body chemistry and health can be damaged by emotional stress and negative attitudes. Selye's book made Cousins think about the possible benefits of positive attitudes and emotions. He thought, "If negative emotions produce (negative) changes in the body, wouldn't positive emotions produce positive chemical changes? Is it possible that love, hope, faith, laughter, confidence, and the will to live have positive therapeutic value?"

3   He decided to concentrate on positive emotions as a remedy to heal some of the symptoms of his ailment. In addition to his conventional medical treatment, he tried to put himself in situations that would elicit positive emotions. "Laugh therapy" became part of his treatment. He scheduled time each day for watching comedy films, reading humorous books, and doing other activities that would bring about laughter and positive emotions. Within eight days of starting his "laugh therapy" program, his pain began to decrease and he was able to sleep more easily. His body chemistry even improved. Doctors were able to see an improvement in his condition! He was able to return to work in a few months' time and actually reached complete recovery after a few years.

4   Skeptical readers may question the doctor's preliminary diagnosis, but Cousins believes his recovery is the result of a mysterious mind-body interaction. His "laugh therapy" is a good example of one of the many alternative, or nonconventional, medical treatments people look to today.

---

[1] *arthritis:* a disease that causes pain and swelling of the joints of the body
[2] *immobilized:* not able to move
[3] *diagnosis:* identification of what illness a person has

Write short answers to these questions.

1. What was Norman Cousins's original diagnosis?

   _____

   _____

2. How did he react, or respond, to his diagnosis?

   _____

   _____

3. What is the connection between mind and body in laugh therapy?

   _____

   _____

4. What are some examples of laugh therapy?

   _____

   _____

5. What was the result of Cousins's laugh therapy?

   _____

   _____

C LINKING READINGS ONE AND TWO

Work in a small group. Discuss these questions. Then choose one of the questions and write your own response.

1. What are the similarities and differences between Norman Cousins's laugh therapy and the Christian Scientists' therapy through prayer and the Bible?

2. Norman Cousins decided to take responsibility for his own health care; he applied laugh therapy. He used an alternative form of treatment to help cure his arthritis, and he was convinced this therapy saved his life. He used his right as an adult to choose the treatment he believed was best for him. Does this right also extend to parents' choice of treatment they believe is best for their child? Why or why not?

3 Focus on Vocabulary

1 *Work with a partner. Write whether the following pairs of words have a similar (S) or different (D) meaning.*

1. doze / sleep _S_

2. symptom / ailment _____

3. persuade / convince _____

4. skeptic / follower _____

5. conventional / alternative _____

6. principles / beliefs _____

7. accuse / defend _____

8. attorney / lawyer _____

9. acknowledge / admit _____

10. shedding / losing _____

11. debate / agreement _____

2 *Read this information about analogies.*

An analogy is a comparison between two words that seem similar or are related in some way. For example, in item 1, *arthritis* is an example of a diagnosis; in the same way, *achiness* is an example of a symptom.

Work with a partner. Discuss the relationship between the words. Circle the letter of the word that best completes each analogy.

1. arthritis : diagnosis :: achiness : _____
   a. disease   **(b.)** symptom   **c.** cure

2. therapy : cure :: treatment : _____
   a. heal   **b.** regimen   **c.** practitioner

3. lawyer : attorney :: doctor : _____
   a. nurse   **b.** patient   **c.** physician

4. typical : common :: unconventional : _____
   a. conventional   **b.** mainstream   **c.** alternative

5. jury : verdict :: doctor : _____
   a. symptom   **b.** diagnosis   **c.** disease

6. medicine : physician :: law : _____
   a. prosecutor   **b.** accuser   **c.** attorney

7. evidence : crime :: symptom : _____
   a. jury   **b.** ailment   **c.** treatment

3 *Imagine that you will interview the Hermansons or Norman Cousins. Write four interview questions that you would like to ask. Use at least one of the words from the box in each question. Exchange questions with a partner and answer your partner's questions as if you were the Hermansons or Norman Cousins.*

symptom	treatment	jury	therapy	lawyer
unconventional	mainstream	physician	accuse	defend
diagnosis	cure	skeptic	achiness	medicine

1. _____

2. _____

3. _____

4. _____

4 Focus on Writing

A GRAMMAR: Past Unreal Conditionals

1 *Work with a partner. Examine the following sentences. Then write true (**T**) or false (**F**) for the statements that follow the sentences.*

a. If Amy <u>hadn't died</u>, the medical examiner <u>wouldn't have examined</u> her.

b. If Amy's parents <u>had seen</u> a conventional doctor, Amy <u>could have taken</u> medicine to control her diabetes.

c. If Amy <u>had sung</u> her favorite song, Mrs. Christman <u>might not have noticed</u> she was sick.

1. In sentence *a:* Amy died. _____

   The medical examiner didn't examine her body. _____

2. In sentence *b:* Amy's parents didn't see a conventional doctor. _____

   Amy didn't take medicine to control her diabetes. _____

3. In sentence *c:* Amy didn't sing her favorite song. _____

   Mrs. Christman didn't notice she was sick. _____

Past Unreal Conditionals

Forming the Past Unreal Conditional

A **past unreal conditional** sentence has two clauses: the *if clause,* which states the condition, and the **result clause,** which states the result. The sentence can begin with either the *if* clause or the result clause and the meaning is the same. Notice the use of the comma (,) when the *if* clause comes at the beginning of the sentence. Notice also the verb forms used in each clause.

If Clause	Result Clause

If + subject + past perfect, subject + *would (not) have* + past participle
$\qquad\qquad\qquad\qquad\qquad\qquad$ *could (not) have*
$\qquad\qquad\qquad\qquad\qquad\qquad$ *might (not) have*

If Amy **hadn't died,**$\quad$ he **would not have examined** her.

Result Clause	*If* Clause

Subject + *would (not) have* + past participle *if* + subject + past participle
$\qquad$ *could (not) have*
$\qquad$ *might (not) have*

Amy **would have taken** medicine $\qquad$ *if* her parents **had brought** her to a doctor.

Using the Past Unreal Conditional

The past unreal conditional talks about past unreal, untrue, or imagined conditions and their results. Both parts of the sentence describe events that are the opposite of what really happened.

Conditional statement: $\qquad$ Mrs. Christman **might not have noticed** if Amy **had sung.**

What really happened: $\qquad$ Mrs. Christman noticed. Amy didn't sing.

The past unreal conditional is often used to express regret about what really happened. To express possibility or uncertainty about the result clause, use *might have* or *could have* in the result clause.

2 *Read the following conditional sentences. Then write true (**T**) or false (**F**) for each statement that follows the sentences.*

1. If Mary Baker Eddy hadn't slipped on the ice, she wouldn't have broken her ankle.

   __T__ She slipped on the ice.

   __F__ She didn't break her ankle.

2. If Norman Cousins had been healthy, he wouldn't have had to try laugh therapy.

   _____ Norman Cousins was healthy.

   _____ He didn't have to try laugh therapy.

3. According to the medical examiner, Amy Hermanson might have lived if she had been given medication.

   _____ Amy died.

   _____ Amy wasn't given medication.

4. If Amy had stayed awake in class, her teacher might not have noticed that something was wrong.

   _____ Amy slept in class.

   _____ Her teacher noticed that something was wrong.

5. If Mary Baker Eddy hadn't been so religious, she might not have turned to prayer to cure herself.

   _____ Mary Baker Eddy was religious.

   _____ She turned to prayer to cure herself.

6. If Amy's parents hadn't been Christian Scientists, they might have gotten conventional medical help for Amy.

   _____ Amy's parents are not Christian Scientists.

   _____ Amy's parents didn't get her conventional medical help.

7. Amy's parents wouldn't have gone on trial for third-degree murder if she had not died.

   _____ Amy's parents didn't go on trial for third-degree murder.

   _____ Amy died.

8. If Norman Cousins hadn't believed in a mind-body interaction, laugh therapy might not have worked for him.

   _____ Norman Cousins didn't believe in a mind-body interaction.

   _____ Laugh therapy didn't work for him.

3 *Write a sentence about each of the following situations. Use the past unreal conditional.*

1. Laurie Rent had a headache. She took some aspirin. She soon felt better.

   If she hadn't taken aspirin, she might not have felt better.

   _____

2. Peter Deering had a problem with his allergies. He used conventional medical treatments. He didn't feel better.

   _____

   _____

3. Norman Cousins read extensively about alternative medicine. When he was diagnosed with ankylosing spondylitis, he already had some ideas about alternative treatments.

   _____

   _____

4. Norman Cousins was sick. He tried to cure himself by using laugh therapy. He soon got better.

   _____

   _____

5. William Bullard was not a Christian Scientist. He believed in conventional Western medicine. He gave his daughter drugs when she was sick.

   _____

   _____

6. Amy began dozing off in class. Her teacher noticed that something was wrong. She called Amy's parents.

   _____

   _____

7. Norman Cousins didn't like his doctor's treatment plan. He developed his own laugh therapy treatment.

   _____

   _____

B   STYLE: Opinion Essays

William and Christine Hermanson were found guilty in the death of their child Amy. They received a four-year suspended sentence and were placed on probation for fifteen years.* The sentence created a great deal of discussion both in favor of and against the verdict. Many people wrote to newspapers expressing their opinion.

1 *Read this opinion essay and discuss the questions with a partner.*

The sentencing of the Hermansons is a shock and a disappointment to me. That any such loving and devoted parents could be convicted of negligence in the death of their children is a mystery. First let me say that I am a loving and devoted parent. I am president of our local parent-teacher association. I am a Harvard graduate and a lawyer. I am a Christian Scientist also. I know that spiritual healing can be an effective treatment, and I would like to share my positive experiences with you.

When I was born, I had a blood problem. The doctor gave me two hours to live. At the time, blood transfusions were not available for this problem. My mother, a Christian Scientist, brought in a practitioner and through much prayer I was healed. I believe that if my mother hadn't been a Christian Scientist, I would probably not have lived. With my own children there have been numerous occasions where conventional medicine would have prescribed antibiotics for ear infections, colds, etc. With the power of prayer, my children have been healed without these medicines.

In the end, I believe that the type of medical treatment chosen should be left up to the individual. Not only is this my opinion, but, in fact, it is a right guaranteed by our Constitution. Choosing the treatment you feel is most effective is a right that cannot be taken away. Children die under medical treatment, too, and no one accuses the parents of negligence or brings them to court.

1. What is the writer's opinion?

2. How does she use her background to support her opinion?

3. What details and examples does she use to support her opinion?

4. What is her conclusion? How does she support her conclusion?

---

* Six years after the Hermansons were found guilty, the Florida Supreme Court overturned the sentencing. The Hermansons were then found innocent of all charges.

Opinion Essays

An **essay** is a piece of writing that includes several paragraphs which are written about the same subject. An **opinion essay** is written to persuade or convince the reader that your opinion is "the right way to think about things."

Organization

An opinion essay includes three parts:

- The **introduction,** which clearly states the opinion of the writer
- The **body** of the essay (one or two paragraphs), which gives examples, details, and facts to support the opinion
- The **conclusion,** which summarizes the arguments in the essay and reinforces the opinion

Audience

When writing an opinion essay, you must think about your audience—your readers—and any opinions or knowledge they already have. If your readers do not have an opinion on the subject, persuading them to agree with you may not be difficult. However, if the audience has an opinion contrary, or opposite, to yours, persuading them may be more challenging. In that case, you must try to convince the readers that at the very least, your opinion is justifiable and worth considering. In order to do this you must present your arguments clearly and support your opinion with evidence: examples, facts, or personal experience.

Supporting Evidence

If you are trying to convince your readers to accept your opinion, you need to give evidence to support your opinion. Also, give reasons which explain why the evidence supports your opinion. Explain why you feel your opinion is correct and the readers' opinions need to be changed.

NOTE: See Units 1 and 2, pages 18–19 and 41–42 for information on paragraph writing.

2 *What is your opinion on the court's initial judgment of the Hermansons? Prepare to write an opinion essay but do not actually write it yet.*

1. Begin by taking a position. Do you support the decision? Why or why not?

2. Complete a chart like the one on page 65. Write notes to introduce, support, and conclude your essay. Use information from the readings and from personal experience.

3. Discuss your outline with a classmate. Is your opinion clearly stated? Do your supporting details really support your position?

THREE MAIN PARTS	
I. Introduction: Clearly state your position/identify your position.	
II. Body: Give details and examples to support your position.	
III. Conclusion: Summarize and reinforce your position.	

C WRITING TOPICS

Write a short opinion essay about one of these topics. Be sure to use some of the ideas, vocabulary, grammar, and style that you have learned in this unit.

1. What is your opinion on the court's initial decision regarding the Hermansons? Use the chart above to guide you as you write.

2. Different cultures define nonconventional medicine in different ways. What do you think nonconventional medicine is? How do you feel about the use of nonconventional medicine?

3. What do you think of Norman Cousins's laugh therapy? Do you think there is any truth to the idea of a mind-body interaction? Have you had a medical experience where your mind was stronger than your body?

D RESEARCH TOPICS

1 *Take a survey of your classmates. Complete the chart on page 66. What do you and your classmates do to help cure the ailments on the chart? List the treatments under conventional or nonconventional. Share your findings with your classmates. Then discuss the questions that follow.*

AILMENT	CONVENTIONAL	NONCONVENTIONAL
Cold		
Cough		
Headache		
Backache		
Stomachache (nausea)		

- Which treatments are most commonly used by your classmates?
- Which treatments do you personally use most often?
- Are there any treatments your classmates use that you would like to try?
- Do you and your classmates have the same ideas about conventional and nonconventional treatment? If not, discuss the differences.

2 *Work in groups. Which treatment would you like to know more about? Brainstorm places to get information. Research the treatment. Share your research with your group. Then write a report including answers to the questions below. Present your report to the class.*

- What is the name of the treatment?
- What does it cure?
- Where does it originate from (for example, a plant, man-made products)?
- Where can you get it (for example, a drugstore, a health food store)?
- Is it commonly used in your country or where you live now? Do you need a doctor's approval to get it?
- How do you take it (for example, a pill, a drink, a compress, a massage)?
- How does it make you feel (for example, tired, dizzy, happy)?

For step-by-step practice in the writing process, see the *Writing Activity Book, High Intermediate,* Unit 3.

Assignment	Opinion essay
Prewriting	Clustering
Organizing	Supporting a thesis statement
Revising	Developing introductions and conclusions
	Using the past unreal conditional
Editing	Formatting an essay

For Unit 3 Internet activities, visit the NorthStar Companion Website at
http://www.longman.com/northstar

When Disaster Strikes

a. Earthquake

b. Dust storm

c. Flood

1 Focus on the Topic

A PREDICTING

Look at the photographs and the title of the unit. Take notes. Then discuss these questions with a partner.

1. What is happening in each of the natural disasters?

2. What problems do you think people will have after the disasters are over?

B SHARING INFORMATION

1 *Work with a partner. Look at the photographs on page 67 and review your notes. What happens in a natural disaster? Match the pictures with some of the common occurrences listed below. Some occurrences may happen during more than one type of disaster.*

_____ sand in your eyes   _____ limited visibility (difficulty seeing)

_____ heavy or strong rain   _____ strong, hot winds

_____ fast-moving clouds   _____ overflowing rivers

_____ trees and limbs of trees   _____ no available drinking water
        breaking and falling

2 *Work with a partner. Look at the map and find the country where you were born. According to the map, what natural disasters have happened near there recently? Do any other natural disasters occur there that are not shown on this map? Have any of these disasters become more common in the past few years? Have you experienced any of these disasters? Discuss.*

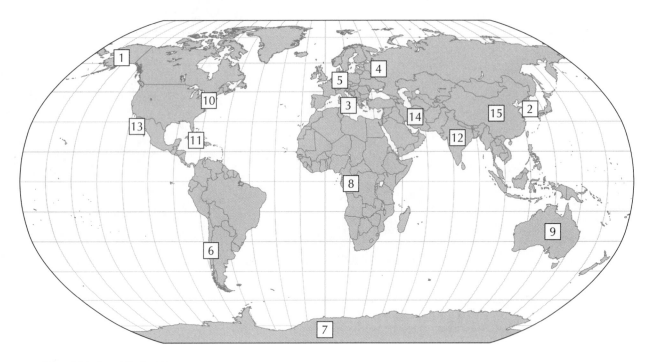

1 Denali National Park, AK, United States: Earthquake, 2002

2 South Korea: Typhoon, 2002

3 Sicily, Italy: Earthquake, 2002

4 Moscow, Russia: Smog, 2002

5 Germany, Austria, Czech Republic, Slovak Republic: Floods, 2002

6 Chile: Landslides, 2002

7 Antarctica: High temperatures, 2002

8 Democratic Republic of the Congo: Volcano eruption, 2002

9 Australia: Brushfires, 2001

10 Buffalo, NY, United States: Severe snowstorm, 2001

11 Cuba: Hurricane, 2001

12 India: Heavy rain, 2001

13 Baja California, Mexico: Hurricane, 2001

14 Iran: Drought, 2001

15 China: Drought, 2001

C   PREPARING TO READ

BACKGROUND

Some scientists believe that changes in our climate in the last century have caused an increase in the number of natural disasters, such as droughts and floods. In 1944 and 1945 in particular, Australia experienced one of the worst droughts in modern history. Large rivers dried up. Land and vegetation dried up and blew away. Drought-related dust storms were frequent. In southeastern Australia, the state of New South Wales was hit hard with dust storms that lasted for hours; some storms lasted for days at a time. Red dust clouds filled the sky. Animals were covered with sand, could not breathe, and eventually died. Houses were filled with sand and dust. Yards were buried in dust. In Mildura, a city near the New South Wales border, four children on the way home from school became disoriented in a strong dust storm and got lost. They weren't rescued until the storm stopped.

Dust storms are accompanied by severe winds containing dust and sand. Imagine you are outside your house and see a dust storm (such as the one in the photo on page 67) approaching. With a partner, talk about how you would prepare for a dust storm.

VOCABULARY FOR COMPREHENSION

Guess the meaning of the underlined words from the context of the following sentences. Circle the letter of the word or phrase that is closest in meaning.

1. One <u>sweltering</u> late afternoon in March, I walked out to collect wood for the stove.
   a. very hot
   b. tiring
   c. pretty

2. A vast <u>boiling</u> cloud was mounting in the sky, black and sulfurous yellow at the heart, varying shades of ocher red at the edges.
   a. lovely
   b. peaceful
   c. growing

3. Where I stood, the air was <u>utterly still</u>, but the writhing cloud was approaching silently and with great speed.
   a. not moving
   b. smelly
   c. clean

4. Always one for action, she turned <u>swiftly</u>, went indoors, and began to close windows.
   a. quietly
   b. painfully
   c. quickly

5. Within the hour, my father arrived home. He and my mother sat on the back step, not in their usual restful contemplation, but silenced by <u>dread</u>.
   a. noise
   b. fear
   c. heat

6. It is dangerous to <u>stray</u> far from shelter, because the sand and grit lodge in one's eyes, and a visibility often reduced to a few feet can make one completely disoriented.
   a. wander
   b. live
   c. sleep

7. Animals which become exhausted and lie down are often sanded over and <u>smothered</u>.
   a. stopped from eating
   b. stopped from breathing
   c. stopped from playing

8. Inside, it is <u>stifling</u>. Every window must be closed against the dust, which seeps relentlessly through the slightest crack.
   a. cold and crowded
   b. hot and airless
   c. wet and dark

9. Meals are <u>gritty</u> and sleep elusive.
   a. infrequent
   b. delicious
   c. dirty

10. The crashing of the <u>boughs</u> of trees against our roof and the sharp roar as a nearly empty tank blew off its stand and rolled away triggered my father's recurring nightmares of France.
    a. branches
    b. leaves
    c. roots

11. The crashing of the boughs of trees against our roof and the sharp roar as a nearly empty tank blew off its stand and rolled away <u>triggered</u> my father's recurring nightmares of France.
    a. shot at
    b. stopped
    c. started

12. "That was only the first storm," he said <u>bleakly</u>. He had seen it all before and knew what was to come.
    a. loudly
    b. slowly
    c. sadly

2 Focus on Reading

A READING ONE: *Drought*

Jill Ker Conway was born in Australia in 1934. Her family lived in remote New South Wales on their sheep farm. They named the farm Coorain, which means "windy place" in the aboriginal language. Unfortunately, Coorain was at the beginning of a great eight-year drought when Conway's family arrived. This excerpt describes a time when the family had gone two years without any substantial rain. In addition, dust storms that originated in the inland desert filled their lives with sand, dust, and dread.

Read the first seven sentences of the reading (until, "We watched helplessly.") and answer the following questions with a partner.

1. What does Jill Ker Conway see?

2. What do you think she tells her mother?

3. What do you think will happen next?

DROUGHT

BY JILL KER CONWAY
(from *The Road from Coorain*)

1   One sweltering late afternoon in March, I walked out to collect wood for the stove. Glancing toward the west, I saw a terrifying sight. A vast boiling cloud was mounting in the sky, black and sulfurous yellow at the heart, varying shades of ocher red at the edges. Where I stood, the air was utterly still, but the writhing[1] cloud was approaching silently and with great speed. Suddenly I noticed that there were no birds to be seen or heard. All had taken shelter. I called my mother. We watched helplessly. Always one for action, she turned swiftly, went indoors, and began to close windows. Outside, I collected buckets, rakes, shovels, and other implements that could blow away or smash a window if hurled against one by the boiling wind. Within the hour, my father arrived home. He and my mother sat on the back step, not in their usual restful contemplation, but silenced by dread.

2   A dust storm usually lasts days, blotting out the sun, launching banshee[2] winds day and night. It is dangerous to stray far from shelter, because the

---

[1] *writhing:* twisting
[2] *banshee:* a loud screaming sound

sand and grit lodge in one's eyes, and a visibility often reduced to a few feet can make one completely disoriented. Animals which become exhausted and lie down are often sanded over and smothered. There is nothing anyone can do but stay inside, waiting for the calm after the storm. Inside, it is stifling. Every window must be closed against the dust, which seeps relentlessly through the slightest crack. Meals are gritty and sleep elusive.[3] Rising in the morning, one sees a perfect outline of one's body, an afterimage of white where the dust had not collected on the sheets.

3   As the winds seared our land, they took away the dry herbage, piled it against the fences, and then slowly began to silt over[4] the debris. It was three days before we could venture out, days of almost unendurable tension. The crashing of the boughs of trees against our roof and the sharp roar as a nearly empty tank[5] blew off its stand and rolled away triggered my father's recurring nightmares of France,[6] so that when he could fall into a fitful slumber[7] it would be to awake screaming.

4   It was usually I who woke him from his nightmares. My mother was hard to awaken. She had, in her stoic way, endured over the years two bad cases of ear infection, treated only with our available remedies, hot packs and aspirin. One ear was totally deaf as a result of a ruptured eardrum, and her hearing in the other ear was much reduced. Now her deafness led to a striking reversal of roles, as I, the child in the family, would waken and attempt to soothe a frantic adult.

5   When we emerged, there were several feet of sand piled up against the windbreak to my mother's garden, the contours of new sandhills were beginning to form in places where the dust eddied[8] and collected. There was no question that there were many more bare patches where the remains of dry grass and herbage had lifted and blown away.

6   It was always a miracle to me that animals could endure so much. As we checked the property, there were dead sheep in every paddock[9] to be sure, but fewer than I'd feared. My spirits began to rise and I kept telling my father the damage was not too bad. "That was only the first storm," he said bleakly. He had seen it all before and knew what was to come.

---

[3] *elusive:* hard to get
[4] *silt over:* to cover with sand and dust
[5] *tank:* a water tank
[6] *France:* refers to Conway's father's participation in World War I, where he witnessed many deaths
[7] *fitful slumber:* restless sleep
[8] *eddied:* moved in circles
[9] *paddock:* a small field where animals are kept

READING FOR MAIN IDEAS

The following sentences are the main ideas from the reading. Number the sentences 1 to 6 to show the correct order in which they appear in the reading. Refer back to the reading if you need help.

_____ Even though some animals survived, this was no time to celebrate because there was more danger to come.

_____ Dust storms are difficult for both animals and people.

_____ The family saw and prepared for the oncoming dust storm.

_____ The sights and sounds of the dust storm were dramatic.

_____ Each member of the family reacted differently to the dust storm.

_____ After the dust storm was over, it was time to assess the damage.

READING FOR DETAILS

Complete the following sentences with details from the reading. Use your own words.

1. After Jill Ker Conway and her mother saw the dust cloud, they each prepared the house and its surroundings for the storm. What exactly did they do?

   Conway _____

   Her mother _____

2. It is dangerous to go outside in a dust storm for many reasons. What are two of them?

   It is dangerous because _____

   It is dangerous because _____

3. During a dust storm, the safest place to be is inside, but even inside it can be very uncomfortable. Why?

   The air _____

   The food _____

   Sleep _____

4. Conway's father had an especially difficult time sleeping. Why?

   While he slept, _____

5. Conway's mother, unlike her father, did not have a problem sleeping.

   She slept well because _____

6. As a result of the storm, the garden had changed. What two changes does Conway mention?

The garden _____

The garden _____

7. Conway and her father had two very different reactions after viewing the damage the storm had done.

Conway _____

Her father _____

REACTING TO THE READING

1 *In the reading, Conway describes the disaster using her senses of sight, hearing, taste, and touch. Look at the reading and find examples of how she describes the disaster using her senses. Complete the chart with the examples. The first one has been started for you.*

SENSE	EXAMPLE FROM READING
Sight	I saw a terrifying sight. A vast boiling cloud was mounting in the sky, black and sulfurous yellow at the heart, varying shades of ocher red at the edges.
Hearing	
Taste	
Touch	

2 *Think of a time when you were in a natural disaster or a big storm. What happened? What effects did the disaster/storm have on your senses? Complete the sentences below with your memories. Then share your answers with a partner. Note that you may not have an entry for each sense.*

The disaster/storm was _____

   I saw _____

   _____

   I heard _____

   _____

   I smelled _____

   _____

   I tasted _____

   _____

   I felt _____

   _____

B READING TWO: *Monologue of Isabel Watching It Rain in Macondo*

In this piece of fiction by Nobel Prize winner Gabriel García Márquez, the character, Isabel, describes the rainfall at the beginning of what will eventually be an enormous flood.

Discuss these questions with a partner.

1. What is a flood?

2. What happens when there is a flood?

3. What would you have to do to prepare for a flood? What would you do during a flood? What do you do after a flood?

MONOLOGUE OF ISABEL WATCHING IT RAIN IN MACONDO

BY GABRIEL GARCÍA MÁRQUEZ
(from *Leaf Storm and Other Stories*)

1   It rained all afternoon in a single tone. In the uniform[1] and peaceful intensity you could hear the water fall, the way it is when you travel all afternoon on a train. But without our noticing it, the rain was penetrating too deeply into our senses. Early Monday morning, when we

5   closed the door to avoid the cutting, icy draft that blew in from the courtyard, our senses had been filled with rain. And on Monday morning they had overflowed. My stepmother and I went back to look at the garden. The harsh gray earth of May had been changed overnight into a dark, sticky substance like cheap soap. A trickle of water began to

10   run off the flowerpots. "I think they had more than enough water during the night," my stepmother said. And I noticed that she had stopped smiling and that her joy of the previous day had changed during the night into a lax and tedious seriousness. "I think you're right," I said. "It would be better to have the Indians put them on the veranda until it

15   stops raining." And that was what they did, while the rain grew like an immense tree over the other trees. My father occupied the same spot where he had been on Sunday afternoon, but he didn't talk about the rain. He said: "I must have slept poorly last night because I woke up with a stiff back." And he stayed there, sitting by the railing with his

20   feet on a chair and his head turned toward the empty garden. Only at dusk, after he had turned down[2] lunch, did he say: "It looks like it will never clear." And I remembered the months of heat. I remembered August, those long and awesome siestas in which we dropped down to die under the weight of the hour, our clothes sticking to our bodies,

25   hearing outside the insistent and dull buzzing of the hour that never passed. I saw the washed-down walls, the joints of the beams all puffed up by the water. I saw the small garden, empty for the first time and the jasmine bush against the wall, faithful to the memory of my mother. I saw my father sitting in a rocker, his painful vertebrae resting on a pil-

30   low and his sad eyes lost in the labyrinth[3] of the rain. I remembered the August nights in whose wondrous silence nothing could be heard except the millenary[4] sound that the earth makes as it spins on its rusty, unoiled axis. Suddenly I felt overcome by an overwhelming sadness.

[1] *uniform:* constant
[2] *turned down:* refused, declined
[3] *labyrinth:* maze, tangle
[4] *millenary:* thousands of years old

Answer these questions with a partner.

1. What does Isabel mean by "our senses had been filled with rain"?

2. Why does Isabel remember August?

3. Why do you think Isabel is so sad?

C LINKING READINGS ONE AND TWO

1 *The two readings are about two families experiencing different disasters, but there are many parallels. Many of the experiences are similar. Complete the chart. Compare the parallel themes between the readings.*

	READING ONE	READING TWO
1. What is the disaster?		
2. What is there too much or not enough of?		
3. What are the effects of the disaster on the house and the surroundings?		
4. How does each character deal with the disaster? What actions do they take? How do you think they feel about the storm?	*The mother*	*The stepmother*
	The daughter	*The daughter*
	The father	*The father*

2 *Using the information in the chart above, write a short paragraph discussing the similarities between the two readings. Focus on the disaster and the people involved.*

3 Focus on Vocabulary

1 *Read this information about adjectives.*

The boldfaced words are adjectives. Many adjectives are formed by combining a base word with a suffix (overwhelm + *-ing* = overwhelming).

- Suddenly I felt overcome by an **overwhelm<u>ing</u>** sadness.
- A visibility often reduced to a few feet can make one completely **disorient<u>ed</u>**.
- I saw my father sitting in a rocker, his **pain<u>ful</u>** vertebrae resting on a pillow and his sad eyes lost in the labyrinth of the rain.

Common adjective suffixes

–al	–ous	–ful	–able	–ive
–ed	–ant	–ic	–ing	–ent

The readings in this unit include many adjectives. Complete the chart with adjectives from the two readings. The third column gives a synonym for the adjective you need to find in the reading. The adjectives are in the order that they are found in the paragraphs or lines noted. Share your answers with the class.

READING	PARAGRAPH OR LINE	FIND AN ADJECTIVE THAT IS A SYNONYM FOR:	ADJECTIVE
1	Paragraph 1	very hot	*sweltering*
1	Paragraph 1	scary	
1	Paragraph 1	quiet; calm	
1	Paragraph 2	not safe	
1	Paragraph 2	very tired	
1	Paragraph 3	extremely difficult	
1	Paragraph 4	nervous	
2	Line 1	calm	
2	Line 13	long and tiring	
2	Line 25	continual; never ending	
2	Line 31	incredible or amazing	
2	Line 33	very large or great	

2 *Work with a partner. Look at the adjectives below. Discuss their meanings. Which adjectives can be used to describe the nouns around them? Write the adjectives next to the nouns, then add more adjectives of your own. Note that many of the adjectives can be used with more than one noun.*

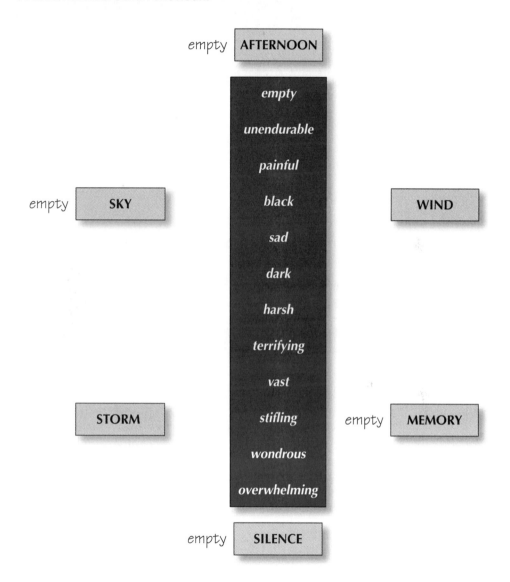

empty **AFTERNOON**

empty

unendurable

painful

empty **SKY**   *black*   **WIND**

sad

dark

harsh

terrifying

vast

STORM   *stifling*   empty **MEMORY**

wondrous

overwhelming

empty **SILENCE**

3 *In both readings, the authors discuss the feeling of helplessness that occurs during a natural disaster. Go back to exercise 2 on page 75. Use your sentences to write a paragraph about it. Describe what it felt like to be overwhelmed by nature. Use at least five adjectives from the two vocabulary exercises above. Include images from exercise 2, page 75.*

4 Focus on Writing

A GRAMMAR: Identifying Adjective Clauses

1 *Examine the following sentences. Then discuss the questions with a partner.*

    a. I collected buckets, rakes, shovels, and other implements <u>that could blow away or smash a window</u>.

    b. My father occupied the same spot <u>where he had been on Sunday afternoon</u>.

    c. Animals <u>which become exhausted and lie down</u> are often sanded over and smothered.

1. In sentence *a*, what kinds of implements is the writer describing?

2. In sentence *b*, which spot is the writer describing?

3. In sentence *c*, are all the animals often sanded over and smothered? If not, which animals are?

4. What words begin the underlined phrases? What words come just before these phrases?

Identifying Adjective Clauses

Identifying adjective clauses, sometimes called restrictive relative clauses, are groups of words (phrases) that act like adjectives to describe or identify a noun. These phrases come directly after the nouns they describe. The adjective clauses begin with relative pronouns that refer to the noun being described. Sentences with adjective clauses can be seen as a combination of two shorter sentences talking about the same noun.

    I lived in **a house.** + **The house** was destroyed by a dust storm.
    = I lived in **a house that was destroyed** by a dust storm.

    The house was very old. + The dust storm destroyed **the house.**
    = **The house that the dust storm destroyed** was very old.

Relative Pronouns

Identifying adjective clauses begin with a relative pronoun. The noun it describes determines the choice of pronoun.

    who for a person or people

    which for a thing or things

    that for a thing or things (less formal than *which* or *who*)

> **when** for a time or times
>
> **where** or **in which** for a place or places
>
> **whose** or **in whose** for possession
>
> **GRAMMAR TIP:** Remember that the relative pronoun takes the place of the noun it describes; the noun is not repeated.
>
> > I lived in **the town**. + The hurricane destroyed **the town**.
> > = I lived in **the town *that*** a hurricane destroyed.

2 *Complete the sentences with the correct relative pronoun.*

1. The firefighter _____who_____ helped save my family was given a
   (which/who)
   medal for heroism.

2. The town _____ I had lived the year before was destroyed by
   (that/where)
   a dust storm.

3. As she sat on the veranda _____ protected her from the
   (which/who)
   torrential rainfall, she reflected on her life.

4. I have a friend _____ house was damaged by Hurricane
   (whose/which)
   Andrew.

5. The hospital _____ I was born was destroyed by the volcano.
   (that/in which)

6. I was asleep at the time _____ the earthquake struck.
   (where/when)

7. The people had to evacuate the village when the dam _____
   (who/that)
   held back the lake broke.

8. Snowstorms _____ happen early in the season often are the
   (in which/that)
   most devastating because people are not prepared.

9. Many people _____ lived on the side of the mountain refused
   (which/who)
   to leave their homes during the avalanche.

10. The house _____ we had slept the night before was
    (where/when)
    completely destroyed by the hurricane.

3 *Combine each pair of sentences into one sentence by using an identifying adjective clause.*

1. **a.** His home was destroyed by the hurricane.

   b. The hurricane came through last night.

   His home was destroyed by the hurricane that came through last night.

   _____

2. **a.** Forest fires kill many animals.

   b. Animals live in national parks.

   _____

   _____

3. **a.** We found the mountain climber.

   b. She had gotten lost during the storm.

   _____

   _____

4. **a.** My flight was canceled because of the storm.

   b. The storm dropped 32 inches of snow on the city.

   _____

   _____

5. **a.** The avalanche occurred at night.

   b. The avalanche trapped the climbers.

   _____

   _____

6. **a.** I spoke with a man.

   b. The man survived the drought of 1944–45.

   _____

   _____

7. **a.** The house had been in Mary's family for over 200 years.

   b. The flood destroyed the house.

   _____

   _____

8. **a.** I saw my friend.

   b. We stayed in her basement during the tornado.

   _____

   _____

9. **a.** The reporter was hit by lightning.

   b. The reporter wrote a story about Hurricane Andrew.

   _____

   _____

10. **a.** The afternoon was sunny and hot.

    b. That afternoon the forest fire broke out.

    _____

    _____

B STYLE: Descriptive Writing

1 *Read each pair of sentences. Circle the letter of the sentence that most effectively describes the situation. With a partner, discuss why you think those sentences are more effective.*

1. **a.** One afternoon in March, I walked out to collect wood for the stove.
   b. One sweltering late afternoon in March, I walked out to collect wood for the stove.

2. **a.** A vast boiling cloud was mounting in the sky, black and sulfurous yellow at the heart, varying shades of ochre red at the edges.
   b. A cloud that had many different colors was building in the sky.

3. **a.** The harsh gray earth of May had been changed overnight into a dark, sticky substance like cheap soap.
   b. The color of the earth had changed from one color to another color.

4. **a.** We closed the door because it was very cold and the wind was coming in from outside.
   b. We closed the door to avoid the cutting, icy draft that blew in from the courtyard.

Descriptive Writing

Descriptive writing makes the reader's senses come alive. It helps the reader see, smell, hear, taste, or feel what is being described. Authors write more descriptively by using adjectives, adjective clauses, and similes.

Adjectives

Adjectives describe nouns. Adjectives can also further describe other adjectives. Notice how adding an adjective gives important information about the noun.

Without Adjective

- I, the child in the family, would soothe an adult.
- He and my mother sat on the step.
- I saw my father sitting in a rocker, his vertebrae resting on a pillow.
- One afternoon in March.

With Adjective

- I, the child in the family, would soothe a **frantic** adult.
- He and my mother sat on the **back** step.
- I saw my father sitting in a rocker, his **painful** vertebrae resting on a pillow.
- One **sweltering late** afternoon in March.

Adjective Clauses

Section 4A explains how an adjective clause acts as an adjective; it gives more information about the noun. For example, in the following sentence excerpt, the relative clause *that never passed* describes the noun, *hour*.

… hearing outside the insistent and dull buzzing of the hour **that never passed.**

Similes

A **simile** creates images by using *"like … "* or *"as … "* to compare two otherwise unrelated ideas. For example, notice how Márquez describes the way the color and substance of the earth changed, using the color and feel of inexpensive soap.

The harsh gray earth of May had been changed overnight into a dark, sticky substance **like cheap soap**.

He also uses the simile of a large tree to describe the growing rain.

… while the rain grew **like an immense tree** over the other trees.

Other Descriptive Phrases

- *Look* and *looked like* are other phrases used to describe a situation or feeling. They give the reader the same impression or experience the writer had.

"It **looks like** it will never clear."

- *As if* and *as though* can be used in the same way as *look like*.

"It looks **as if** it will never clear." (or "It *looked* **as if** it *would* never clear.")

"It looks **as though** it will never clear." (or "It *looked* **as though** it *would* never clear.")

2 *Add adjectives to the underlined nouns to make the following sentences more descriptive.*

1. I looked up and saw a <u>dust cloud</u>.

_____

2. The <u>rain</u> that started on Saturday never stopped.

_____

3. We drank the <u>water</u> even though we knew it might have been contaminated.

_____

4. The <u>winds</u> that came with the hurricane took the roof off the house.

_____

5. The <u>earth</u> blew away in a large dust storm.

_____

6. We spent an <u>afternoon</u> waiting and waiting for it to stop raining.

_____

3 *Add a word or phrase from the box to each phrase below. Then add your own description to make a complete sentence.*

as	as if	look
like	as though	looked like

1. During the drought the ground was *as dry as a bone* _____ .

2. The wind and rain penetrated our house _____

_____ .

3. The tornado was approaching quickly. It sped through the sky _____

_____ .

4. The storm screeched through the night. It sounded _____

_____ .

5. When the storm finally stopped we went outside. It _____

_____ .

C WRITING TOPICS

Write an essay about one of these topics. Be sure to use some of the ideas, vocabulary, grammar, and style that you have learned in this unit.

1. Think about a time when you were in a natural disaster. Refer back to exercise 1 on page 74 and describe how the disaster affected your senses.

2. Think about a time when you felt very scared or helpless. Describe in detail the event and how it affected you physically and emotionally.

3. Look at the photographs on page 67. Choose a photo and imagine you are in the disaster. Describe your physical and emotional feelings.

D RESEARCH TOPIC

Investigate a natural disaster.

Step 1: Work in a small group. Brainstorm a list of famous natural disasters from ancient times through the present day.

Step 2: Share your list with the class and make a master list of disasters on the chalkboard. Discuss the disasters and what you know about them.

Step 3: Work in a small group. Select one disaster for your group to research and discuss where you will find information.

Step 4: Research the natural disaster your group selected and prepare a report that includes the following information. Present your report to the class.

- Date, type, and description of disaster

- Visuals of the disaster (photos, drawings, paintings)

- Aftermath (what happened as a result of the disaster; for example, an amazing survival story, a description of the damages and losses)

- Statistics (people injured or killed, monetary amount of damage)

For step-by-step practice in the writing process, see the *Writing Activity Book, High Intermediate,* Unit 4.

Assignment	Narrative essay
Prewriting	Categorizing
Organizing	Creating a narrative
Revising	Writing descriptions
	Using identifying adjective clauses
Editing	Correcting comma splices

For Unit 4 Internet activities, visit the NorthStar Companion Website at
http://www.longman.com/northstar

UNIT **5**

21st-Century Living

1 Focus on the Topic

A PREDICTING

Look at the photograph and the title of the unit. Then discuss these questions with a partner.

1. What does the photograph show?

2. How do you think this area looked 30 years ago? How do you think it will look 30 years from now?

3. Why do you think changes like this occur?

B SHARING INFORMATION

Interview three classmates. Ask them the following questions about the town or city they are from. Share their answers with the class.

1. Where are you from?

2. What is the population?

3. Is the population increasing or decreasing? Why is this happening?

4. What changes, if any, have you seen over the years as the result of the change in population?

C PREPARING TO READ

BACKGROUND

Look at the map below. The cities in the map are megacities. A megacity is a city with a population of over 10 million people. These megacities and many other cities are growing daily. More than 50 percent of the world's population now lives in cities. Megacities are a result of urban sprawl. The term "urban sprawl" describes cities that grow outward and take over surrounding agricultural (farm) land.

Population Growth and Projections

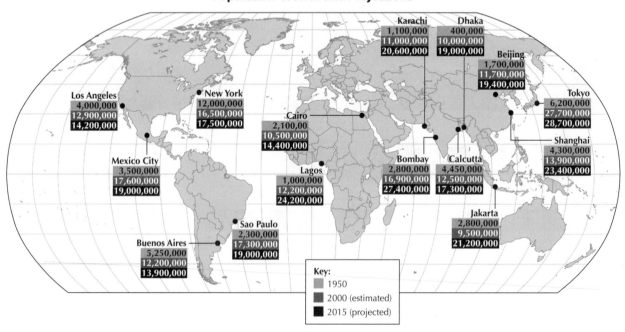

Now, look at the drawing of an integral neighborhood, or ecovillage. Ecovillages are developed by urban planners trying to find ways to control urban sprawl and its negative consequences. Neighborhoods like this encourage local energy and food production, conservation of resources, neighborhood businesses, and an overall sense of community involvement and care.

Work with a partner. Try to find at least seven community and environmentally friendly characteristics of the ecovillage. Share your findings with the class.

VOCABULARY FOR COMPREHENSION

Read the information about environmental problems. Then write each underlined word beside its synonym below.

When our grandparents were children, people had very little awareness of environmental problems. They should have been more environmentally conscious, but they might not have believed there would be a shortage of natural <u>resources</u> such as wood, water, or oil. However, today people all over the world are facing the realization that our natural resources are limited.

What is the <u>root</u> cause of this shortage? One of the causes is our stubborn dependence on cars powered by <u>fossil fuels</u>. Our <u>sprawling</u> cities force us to drive miles and miles every day to satisfy our daily needs. <u>Clogged</u> highways and traffic jams are proof that we are overly dependent on automobiles.

How can we solve this problem? Some urban planners are designing *ecocities,* cities that are compact, <u>convenient</u>, and environmentally friendly. These cities will have easy access to <u>efficient</u> public transportation, as well as bicycle and pedestrian walking paths. In addition, these communities will be <u>sustainable</u>. They will not simply rob the earth of resources in order to exist. They will <u>incorporate</u> solar and wind-powered energy rather than relying solely on fossil fuels. Residents will be able to grow fruits and vegetables in community gardens and indoor solariums. These cities will also have green spaces, parks, and forests, providing a natural <u>habitat</u> for wildlife survival and human relaxation. Furthermore, they will be built with recycled materials and wood from certified sustainable forestry operations. By incorporating all of these features into ecocities, urban planners believe we will be able to start <u>restoring</u> our environment so there will be something left for our grandchildren.

a. _____*incorporate*_____ include

b. _____ surroundings

c. _____ supplies

d. _____ congested; overcrowded

e. _____ bringing back

f. _____ basic

g. _____ easily accessible

h. _____ competent and without waste

i. _____ expansive

j. _____ coal, oil, or natural gas

k. _____ able to use resources without depleting or damaging them

2 Focus on Reading

A   READING ONE: *Cities Against Nature*

Innovative and forward-thinking urban planners (people who design and plan cities) are looking for ways to control urban sprawl and the damage it causes. Urban planners combine the science of ecology[1] with city planning. By combining these two fields of study, planners are able to design and create ecocities. In this reading you will learn about what cities and towns may be like in the future.

Before you read, examine the seven boldfaced section headers in Reading One. Check (✓) the sections where the following information might appear.

SECTION HEADER	WHY PARKS ARE IMPORTANT	ADVANTAGES OF AN ECOCITY	DISCUSSION OF SOLAR OR WIND POWER	MOVING AROUND IN AN ECOCITY
Designing the Cities of Tomorrow				
Urban Ecology				
What's So Great About an Ecocity?				
Transportation Choices: Feet First				
Green and Open Spaces				
Conserving Energy and Resources				
Building Better Cities Around the World				

---

[1] *ecology:* the way in which plants, animals, and people are related to each other and to their environment

CITIES AGAINST NATURE

BY NANCY BRUNING
(from *Cities Against Nature*)

Designing the Cities of Tomorrow

1   It's clear that something is wrong with most of today's cities. They waste resources; they pollute our air, our water, and our minds, or relationships with other people; and they hurt animals and plants.

2   What kind of future do we want? Should it include cities at all? We need to give thought to those places that more than half of the world's population calls home.

3   It makes sense to work on our cities because, first of all, so many of them already exist. That's just as well because today there are so many people in the world that if we all lived in the country, there wouldn't be any country. The world would be one gigantic sprawling suburb.

4   Besides, cities have a lot to offer. Some people talk about the "magic" of the city—its creative, lively people; its streets; its theatres, museums, and schools; its excitement and its thrilling pace. The density (number of people per acre) of a city makes it possible for people to learn from each other, to enjoy things together, and to work together.

5   Compact cities do less damage to the environment, per person, than suburbs do. People in cities live close together, using less land. And it's easier and more efficient to provide the services they need—garbage collection, mail delivery, police and fire protection, hospitals.

6   Cities are at the center of human life. They challenge our creativity. They make it more likely that everyone will be heard and treated more fairly. So cities can be the best and biggest tool to help us understand and take better care of the world and each other . . . if we improve the way they are designed.

Urban Ecology

7   The science of ecology deals with the connection between living creatures and the connection between creatures and their environment. Urban ecologists study the connection between the city and everything living in it and between a city and the larger environment that the city itself is a part of.

8   Urban ecologists believe that redesigning cities gives us a chance to get at the root causes of our environmental problems. For example, we have seen how harmful it is to depend on gasoline-powered pollution. If we burned fossil fuel or used nuclear energy to create the electricity, we would just move the pollution from one place to another. Also, we would still have clogged highways and deaths due to traffic accidents. And, we would still use too much land for roads and parking.

9   A greater change would be for people to walk or take public transit. But this is not always practical or even possible, because sprawl spreads things too far apart to create good public transit or walk to most places. A greater change would be to reduce the amount of sprawl—this would improve the air and help take care of other problems.

10   Redesigning our cities into ecocities—cities built on sound ecological principles—will make them better places to live. It will launch changes that reach far beyond cities.

What's So Great About an Ecocity?

11   The ecocity will look to the future, but it will also improve the lives of the people living today. Ecocities are better than today's cities because:

- Instead of wasting resources, the ecocity conserves them and emphasizes the use of renewable resources.
- Instead of polluting our air, water, and soil, the ecocity emphasizes the use of clean, nonpolluting energy sources in agriculture and other industries.
- Instead of hurting our health, the ecocity helps keep us healthy in body and mind.
- Instead of hurting nature, the ecocity exists in balance with nature and considers the needs of plants and other animals as well as those of humans.

Transportation Choices: Feet First

12   Because dependence on cars is at the root of so many urban problems, ecocities will be constructed so that most of us will get around by walking. When a place is too far to reach on foot, the ecocity offers transportation choices that are less harmful to the environment than cars.

13   In ecocities, you will be able to get around easily and safely on bicycles (or skateboards or roller skates) and pubic transit. The public transit system might include buses, light-rail lines (like trolleys), ferries, and trains. They will be coordinated, with more frequent service, and with easy transfer between types of transportation. It will be safer, more affordable, and more convenient to use than cars.

Green and Open Spaces

14   Cities today were often built in ways that covered or destroyed hills, creeks, shorelines, and open spaces. Ecocities will incorporate, preserve, and restore such natural and recreational resources.

15   Experts believe we need to establish a greenbelt—a housing-free zone around the cities to protect natural areas and farms. The greenbelt would have permanent boundaries within which no further development would be allowed. This would preserve existing habitats for migrating and permanent birds, and other wildlife, as well as agricultural land, ranches, forests, recreation areas and parks, and wilderness areas.

Conserving Energy and Resources

16   Ecocities will save energy and resources in many ways. The biggest way, of course, is that they rely more on "people power" for transportation than on cars. Public transportation also uses energy and materials much more efficiently than private cars. So just getting us out of our cars will save a tremendous amount.

17   In addition, ecocities will use a minimum of fossil fuels for other purposes. Instead, they will rely on renewable and less polluting energy sources such as solar power, biomass (plant and animal waste used for fuel), hydrogen, and wind power. They will even have hydroelectric-power–driven dams that will be small enough not to harm the environment.

18   Ecocity buildings are heated and kept cool more efficiently. They use more efficient motors to get work done, and they use energy-efficient lighting and appliances. They take advantage of the sun's natural ability to heat a space when heat is needed. They also take advantage of cooling breezes, open windows, window shades, and trees and shrubs to reduce heat from direct sunlight. Whenever possible, ecocity buildings will be made from local materials.

Building Better Cities Around the World

19   Ecocities sound pretty good, don't they? Although no complete ecocities exist yet, there are hints that someday they will show up all over the world. A growing group of environmentalists, architects, city and regional planners, transportation experts, elected officials, scientists, ordinary concerned citizens, and young people are taking the first steps towards changing the way we build and live in our cities.

20   They are aiming to make our cities sustainable, which means that they don't take anything away from the Earth's environment, so that the next generation, and the next, will not find a deteriorated planet.

21   There are two basic ways of creating ecocities—building brand-new ones, "from scratch" and reshaping cities that already exist. It's harder but more important to reshape existing cities. That way, we use a minimum of land and resources, and more people will be able to stay in the community they live in now.

READING FOR MAIN IDEAS

Complete the following statements about each section of the reading.

1. Designing the Cities of Tomorrow

Today's cities have a lot to offer; they just need _____

_____

_____

2. Urban Ecology

    Urban ecologists must design cities thinking about _____

    _____

    _____

3. What's So Great About an Ecocity?

    An ecocity protects people and the environment by _____

    _____

    _____

4. Transportation Choices: Feet First

    Ecocities stress public transportation and walking because _____

    _____

    _____

5. Green and Open Spaces

    Instead of destroying nature, ecocities _____

    _____

    _____

6. Conserving Energy and Resources

    By using alternative non-polluting energy resources, ecocities will _____

    _____

    _____

7. Building Better Cities Around the World

    Cities must be sustainable so they _____

    _____

    _____

READING FOR DETAILS

The reading describes many of the positive and negative effects that cities and the people who live in them have on the environment. Complete the chart with the effects related to the cause listed. Circle (+) if the effect is positive or (–) if the effect is negative.

CAUSE	EFFECT
Large cities	+ ⊖ *waste resources* + ⊖ *pollute the air, water, and soil* ⊕ – *creative, exciting places to live*
Compact cities	+ – + – + –
Dependence on cars	+ – + –
Walking and public transportation	+ – + –
Redesigning cities	+ – + –
Creating greenbelts	+ – + –
Relying on renewable resources for heat and electricity	+ – + –

REACTING TO THE READING

1 *Imagine you are an urban planner who is converting an existing city into a more environmentally friendly city. You are at a local meeting of concerned citizens. Your plan is being questioned. Read the following statements and respond to them.*

1. "I've had a car for over 30 years. I don't want to have to walk now. It's inconvenient."

_____

_____

2. "I don't want to have to rely on solar power. What if it's a cloudy day?"

_____

_____

3. "Are you asking me to give up my appliances and lights?"

_____

_____

4. "It sounds expensive."

_____

_____

5. "We have parks already. Why do we need more green spaces?"

_____

_____

6. "It sounds like you want us to build a whole new city. I like my house and neighborhood."

_____

_____

2 _Work in small groups. Imagine that you and your classmates are urban planners. Think about the community where you are living now. What suggestions can you make to improve your community? Review the suggestions and ideas for ecocities in Reading One. Which of the suggestions would be possible for your community? How could they work? Share your ideas with the class._

B | READING TWO: *Earthship Homes Catch Old Tires on Rebound*

Some innovative architects and citizens are designing new homes as eco-homes or ecologically friendly homes. These new houses are built with the same sound ecological principles as ecocities. They are self-sufficient and try to lessen the negative impact on the environment.

Work with a partner. Look at the picture and discuss these questions.

1. Do you think this home looks comfortable?

2. Would you like to live here? Why or why not?

3. This home is very special. Can you guess why?

4. Why do you think it is called an "earthship"?

An earthship home

Earthship Homes Catch Old Tires on Rebound

By Eva Ferguson (from the *Calgary Herald*)

1   They're called earthships—an environmentalist's dream home made from up to 2,000 scrap tires, packed dirt, straw and concrete.

2   From the outside each looks like a berm[1] with a solarium in front. On the inside, it can be a luxurious mansion for everyday living or just a cozy one-room cabin with a great view.

3   Hundreds have been built in the U.S. Midwest for a wide range of homeowners, including environmentally conscious celebrities such as Dennis Weaver[2] and low-income earners who want homes made of cheap materials and no heating bills—thanks to solar heating.

4   A handful of earthships are under construction in British Columbia [Canada] and now a Calgary entrepreneur is anxious to build them in Canmore, Crossfield, Exshaw [Alberta, Canada] or any remote area where Albertans are willing to try something unique that helps the environment too.

5   "Because the homes are totally self-sufficient, they're very affordable, and it's a way to get rid of used tires which have been such a headache for years" [said

[1] ***berm:*** a pile or bank of earth placed against the wall of a building to provide protection and warmth
[2] ***Dennis Weaver:*** an American actor

Michael Port]. In support of reusing old tires, Alberta's tire recycling management board launched the Recycling Industry Incentive Program, which provides up to $2 per tire for projects that use scrap tires in innovative ways.

6　To build a modest earthship, about 2,000 tires are stacked up atop each other and packed with dirt, straw, and cement to make up the main frame. An average sized home takes up to 90 to 135 square meters [295 to 443 square feet]. The front, which faces south for maximum sunlight, is a solarium made of large glass windows. Because the earth and rubber from the tires trap heat, heating is never required, even in cold climates such as Alberta's. Ultimately the tires are completely covered, by drywall on the inside and earth on the outside. Solariums provide a great opportunity for gardens as well, allowing owners to grow their own vegetables at home.

7　Utilities like water, sewage, and electricity do not have to come from municipal sources. Running water and sewage storage is handled through underground tanks. "Photovoltaic" lights, which store solar energy in their own batteries, provide lighting at night. But for those who can't be without their TVs or microwaves, electricity can be installed.

8　Michael Reynolds, owner of Solar Survival Architecture, which initiated the idea and started successful construction in New Mexico, Colorado, and Idaho just a few years ago, said the homes are becoming popular in Japan, Australia, Europe, and South America.

9　"Housing itself is difficult to come by.[3] Many people practically have to sell their souls to buy one. But these are affordable because they're made with old automobile tires, they don't create heating or cooling bills, and owners can even participate in their construction if they like."

10　The total price can range from $30,000 to $1 million, depending on size and amenities, he said.

[3] *come by:* to obtain

Reprinted with the permission of the *Calgary Herald*.

In your own words, write a brief description of an earthship home. Share your description with the class.

C　LINKING READINGS ONE AND TWO

1　*The principles of ecocities and earthship homes are very similar. Look at the chart on page 100. The first column lists some of the principles of ecocities from Reading One. Complete the second column with examples from Reading Two showing how earthship homes are also built based on the same ecological principles.*

ECOCITIES	EARTHSHIP HOMES
Ecocites exist in balance with nature.	*Earthship homes are built into the natural landscape. They are situated to take advantage of natural sunlight.*
Ecocities use a minimum of fossil fuels.	
Ecocity buildings are heated and kept cool more efficiently.	
Ecocity buildings are made from local materials.	
Ecocities try to be sustainable communities.	

2 *Earthships are increasing in popularity every year. There are now thousands of earthship homes in countries all over the world including Scotland, England, Mexico, Chile, Bolivia, Japan, Belgium, South Africa, and Russia. In addition, many existing cities worldwide are incorporating eco-friendly features. Are people living in earthship homes committed to the local environment on a different level than people living in ecocities? If yes, how and in what ways?*

3 Focus on Vocabulary

1 *Complete the sentences with the correct form of the words given. If you need help, use a dictionary. Check your answers with a partner.*

1. create, creative, creativity

   a. In order to plan an ecocity, an urban planner must use a lot of ___creativity___.

   b. Earthship homes are one example of a ___creative___ solution to the problem of dwindling natural resources.

   c. Some people believe that for the planet to survive, we must ___create___ only ecocities in the future.

2. environment, environmental, environmentally, environmentalist

    a. An _____ is someone who is concerned about protecting the environment.

    b. Environmentalists believe that compact cities do less damage to the _____, per person, than suburbs do.

    c. We cannot solve our _____ problems without looking at their causes.

    d. Earthship homes are more _____ friendly than traditional homes; they cause less pollution.

3. ecology, ecocity, ecologists, ecological

    a. The science of _____ deals with the connection between living creatures and the connection between creatures and their environment.

    b. By minimizing the use of fossil fuels and therefore pollution, we do less _____ damage to the environment.

    c. A city built using sound ecological principles is an _____.

    d. _____ study the way in which plants, animals, and people are related to each other and to their environment.

4. efficient, efficiently, efficiency

    a. Buildings in ecocities, similar to earthship homes, use energy more _____ than traditional homes and buildings.

    b. These homes use _____ lighting and heating.

    c. Builders are trying to think of ways to improve the _____ of homes.

5. construction, constructed, constructive

    a. There are many _____ actions we can take to improve our environment.

    b. Earthship homes are now being _____ on all continents except Antarctica.

    c. The _____ of an earthship home costs between $30,000 and $1,000,000.

2 *Using some of the vocabulary from exercise 1 on pages 100–101, complete the following letter to the editor.*

To the Editor:

As we enter the new millennium, people seem to be more and more concerned with the (1)_____. We read and hear about many problems including global warming, dwindling natural resources, and pollution. But what can we do to solve these problems? Is it too late?

Ecocities are one of the solutions that (2)_____ have come up with to solve these growing (3)_____ problems. In order for these cities to be successful, urban planners must be (4)_____. Ecocities must be compact because compact cities do less harm to the environment. Ecocities must also use energy in an (5)_____ manner in order to minimize use of fossil fuels and lessen pollution. All of this is great if you happen to live near an ecocity, but what can the average individual do to be (6)_____ conscious?

One solution some people have found is to build earthship homes. You don't have to be an urban planner or rich to (7)_____ an earthship home. They can be (8)_____ for as little as US$30,000 using recycled tires, and the owners are even able to participate in their (9)_____. In addition, they use energy (10)_____.

I have lived in an earthship home for five years. In fact, I built it myself. Living in an earthship home is a continual reminder that individuals can make and do make a difference.

–From a concerned citizen and earthship home owner

3 *Read this information.*

Many people now believe that the time has come for us to rethink the way in which we live. We must learn to reuse, reduce, and recycle our waste. We must also create ways to make our energy burn cleaner and more efficiently. In this unit, you have read about some solutions to these issues at both the community and individual level.

Using ten of the words from exercise 1 on pages 100–101, respond to one of the following questions.

1. Some communities have already begun implementing eco-friendly solutions similar to those in the two readings. Have you seen or read about any communities that are taking eco-friendly actions to improve or maintain the environment? Write a paragraph discussing these solutions.

2. Think about a city you know well. Propose a plan to make the city more eco-friendly. Be specific in your ideas and solutions. Present your proposal to the class.

4 Focus on Writing

A GRAMMAR: Advisability and Obligation in the Past

1 *Examine the following sentence and answer the question.*

Urban planners <u>should have designed</u> ecocities sooner.

What does the sentence mean?
a. Urban planners wanted to design ecocities sooner than they did.
b. Urban planners needed to design ecocities sooner, but they didn't.

Advisability and Obligation in the Past

To talk about actions that were advisable in the past, use the modals **should have, could have, ought to have,** and **might have.**

Forming Past Modals

Modal	+	*Have*	+	Past Participle
could		have		designed
should (not)		have		seen
might		have		changed
ought (not) to		have		built

(continued)

Using Past Modals to Express Regret

Past modals can express regret about past possibilities and actions not taken.

Situation: I built a house that is not energy-efficient.
Expressing regret: I **ought to have built** an earthship home.

Situation: I threw away all my bottles and cans in the trash.
Expressing regret: I **could have recycled** them instead.

Situation: I drove my car in the city and got stuck in a traffic jam.
Expressing regret: I **shouldn't have driven** my car. I **should have taken** public transportation.

Using Past Modals to Express Blame

Past modals can also express blame. The blame is based on your opinion of a situation.

Situation: Our governments have let big businesses pollute our air for a long time.
Expressing blame: Our governments **should not have allowed** big businesses to continue to pollute for so many years.

GRAMMAR TIP: *Ought not to have* and *should not have* are the only modals used to express advisability and obligation in the past that have negative forms. Both mean the same thing, but *should not have* is more common.

2 *Read the following situations. Write sentences using the past modals given.*

1. Joan drove to the store to get the newspaper. The store was only half a mile away.

   (should not have) *Joan shouldn't have driven to the store.*

   (ought to have) *She ought to have ridden her bicycle.*

2. The urban planners did not include a greenbelt in their plans for the ecocity. Birds and other wildlife disappeared from the city.

   (should not have) _____

   (should have) _____

3. Mr. Andrews used all new tires when he built his earthship.

   (should not have) _____

   (could have) _____

4. Land developers have cut down large sections of rain forests all over the world. Many potential valuable medicines are being destroyed.

(should not have) _____

(ought to have) _____

5. People have thrown hazardous waste materials into landfills for years. Drinking water in many of these areas is now polluted.

(should not have) _____

(might have) _____

6. Last year, a man built an earthship and installed all his windows facing to the north. His house was always cold and his indoor garden was not very successful.

(should not have) _____

(ought to have) _____

3 *Read the following situations. Complete the sentences expressing your opinion (blame or regret) using past modals.*

1. Air pollution is a big problem in many cities because too many people drive cars. Governments in the past should _have built better subway systems._

2. Fourteen billion pounds of garbage were dumped in the world's oceans last year. This garbage might _____

_____

3. Gas and oil costs have continued to rise because the planet is running out of fossil fuels. In the past, people ought to _____

_____

4. Rain forests have been destroyed at an alarming rate. In the past, people should _____

_____

5. Urban sprawl makes good public transportation difficult to implement. In the past, urban planners could _____

_____

B   STYLE: Cause and Effect

1 *Examine the following sentences. Discuss the questions with the class.*

a. Because dependence on cars is at the root of so many problems, ecocities will be constructed so that most of us will get around by walking.

b. They are aiming to make our cities sustainable, so that the next generation, and the next, will not find a deteriorated planet.

c. The homes are totally self-sufficient; consequently, they are very affordable.

d. Because the homes are made with old automobile tires, they are very affordable.

e. Since the earth and rubber trap heat, heating is never required.

1. What is the clause that expresses the cause in each sentence?

2. Can you identify the effect, or result, clause?

3. What words connect the cause and effect clauses?

Cause and Effect

Cause and effect sentences explain why something happened. There are two clauses in a cause and effect sentence. The **cause clause** explains why something happened. The **effect clause** explains the result of what happened.

Cause: Because dependence on cars is at the root of so many problems,

Effect: Ecocities will be constructed for pedestrians.

Subordinating Conjunctions and Transitions

Subordinating conjunctions and transitions show the relationship between the two clauses.

Subordinating Conjunctions Introducing the Cause	Transitions Introducing the Effect
because	as a result
since	consequently
	for this reason
	so
	therefore
	thus

The Cause Clause

- The **cause clause** is introduced by *because* or *since.* When the cause is at the beginning of the sentence, use a comma (,).

  Because dependence on cars is at the root of so many problems, ecocities will be constructed for pedestrians.

- When the cause is at the end of the sentence, do not use a comma.

  Ecocities will be constructed for pedestrians **because dependence on cars is at the root of so many problems.**

The Effect Clause

- The **effect clause** is introduced by words such as *consequently, as a result, for this reason, so, therefore,* and *thus.* Cause and effect clauses can be combined into one sentence by using a semicolon (;) and a comma (,).

  The homes are totally self-sufficient; **consequently, they are very affordable.**

- A sentence with *so* only uses a comma.

  The homes are totally self-sufficient, **so they are very affordable.**

- They can also be two separate sentences.

  The homes are totally self-sufficient. **Consequently, they are very affordable.**

2 *Read the following paragraph. Underline the words in each sentence that introduce the cause and effect clauses. Then, with a partner, complete the chart that follows.*

Houses in the United States are very expensive; as a result, many people have to invest all their savings to buy one. Thankfully, earthship homes are affordable because they are made with old automobile tires. In addition, because they are well insulated, they don't create high heating or cooling bills. Furthermore, since owners can participate in the construction, the cost is controlled.

CAUSE	EFFECT
1. Houses are very expensive.	
2.	Earthship homes are affordable.
3.	
4.	

3 Identify the cause (C) and the effect (E) for each set of sentences. Then combine the sentences with the words given.

1. _C_ Urban sprawl is beginning to threaten our health and well-being.

    _E_ Urban planners are starting to seriously look at ways to improve the way cities are built and managed.

    (so) _Urban sprawl is beginning to threaten our health and well-being, so urban planners are starting to seriously look at ways to improve the way cities are built and managed._

2. ____ The ozone layer is becoming depleted.

    ____ There are more cases of skin cancer every year.

    (therefore) _____

    _____

3. ____ The world's rain forests are rapidly shrinking.

    ____ There will be fewer valuable medicines available.

    (consequently) _____

    _____

4. ____ There are more heat waves and cold snaps.

    ____ Climate changes from global warming are making weather patterns more extreme.

    (as a result) _____

    _____

5. ____ Drinking water near many landfills has become contaminated.

    ____ People have been throwing hazardous waste into landfills for years.

    (because) _____

    _____

6. ____ People have been cutting down large areas of forests.

    ____ Many animal species have become endangered.

    (for this reason) _____

    _____

7. ____ There are more than 500 million cars in the world.

    ____ The atmosphere is increasingly in danger.

    (since) _____

    _____

C WRITING TOPICS

Write an essay about one of the following topics. Be sure to use some of the ideas, vocabulary, grammar, and style that you have learned in this unit.

1. Urban sprawl is a worldwide problem. Paolo Soleri, a famous architect who is designing an ecocity in the state of Arizona in the United States, says:

   "The problem I am confronting is the present design of cities only a few stories high, stretching outward in unwieldy sprawl for miles. As a result of their sprawl, they literally transform the earth, turn farms into parking lots and waste enormous amounts of time and energy transporting people, goods and services over their expanses. My solution is urban implosion rather than explosion."

   Do you agree or disagree with Paolo Soleri's belief that cities should implode (become more compact) in order to conserve land and save energy? Would you be willing to live in a smaller amount of space in order to protect and save the environment?

2. Describe an approach one country has taken to solve an environmental problem. Be sure to explain what has caused the government to take this approach and whether you think it has been successful. Write about what the country should have done to make it more successful or what it can do to continue its success.

3. Global warming is an environmental issue on many people's minds these days. Many scientists blame global warming on the depletion of the ozone layer. One of the causes for the depletion may be due to car emissions. Could governments have done more in the past to prevent this problem? What can governments do now to prevent further damage?

D RESEARCH TOPIC

There are many examples of environmentally friendly building projects around the world. These are called Green Buildings, Sustainable Buildings, Sustainable Communities, EcoCommunities, *or* EcoVillages. *Research an environmentally friendly project or choose one from the list on page 110. Write a report including the following information. Present your report to the class.*

- Name of community or building

- Location

- History

- Philosophy of the builder or community

- Examples of environmentally friendly aspects

Green Projects
Green Building Challenge 2002—Canada

EcoResorts
Harmony Studios Sustainable Resort—St. John, U.S. Virgin Islands

Green Buildings or Sustainable Buildings
Audubon House—New York City, New York, United States
Four Times Square—New York City, New York, United States

EcoCommunities
Pine Street Cohousing—Amherst, Massachusetts, United States

EcoVillages
Crystal Waters Village—Queensland, Australia
Arcosanti—Arcosanti, Arizona, United States

Arcosanti, an ecovillage in Arizona, United States

For step-by-step practice in the writing process, see the *Writing Activity Book, High Intermediate,* Unit 5.

Assignment	Cause and effect essay
Prewriting	Flowcharting
Organizing	Organizing causes and effects
Revising	Introducing the problem and proposing solutions
	Expressing blame and regret with past modals
Editing	Correcting sentence fragments

For Unit 5 Internet activities, visit the NorthStar Companion Website at
http://www.longman.com/northstar

Give and Learn

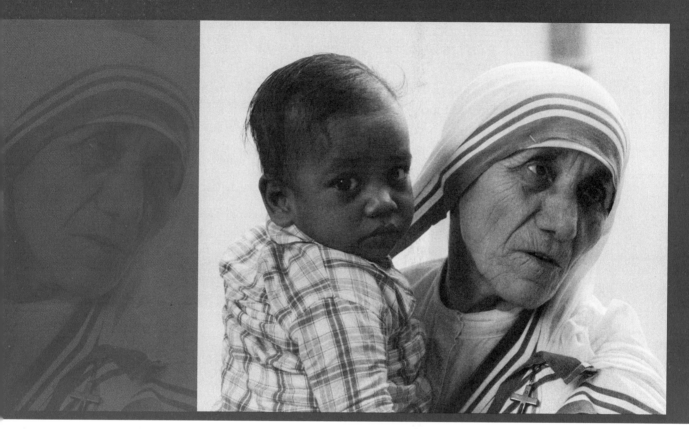

1 Focus on the Topic

A PREDICTING

Look at the photograph of Mother Teresa and the title of the unit. Then discuss these questions with a partner.

1. Philanthropy is a way of showing concern for other people by giving money or volunteering—working without pay—to help needy people or organizations. What are some of the ways that Mother Teresa helped people in need?

2. What do you think the title of the unit means? What do you think this unit will be about?

B SHARING INFORMATION

Work in a small group. The following quotations represent a philosophy, or a certain way of thinking, about philanthropy. Read these statements and answer the questions that follow. Share your ideas with the class.

"It is better to give than to receive."
—Acts 20:35, Bible, Revised Standard Version

"A person's true wealth is the good he or she does in the world."
—Mohammed

"He who bestows[1] his goods upon the poor,
Shall have as much again, and ten times more."
—John Bunyan, *Pilgrim's Progress*, Part Two, Section VII

1. What philosophy is expressed in these quotations?

_____

_____

2. What is an example of this philosophy?

_____

_____

3. Do you know anyone who incorporates this philosophy into his or her life? Describe something this person does.

_____

_____

C PREPARING TO READ

BACKGROUND

Across the United States, more and more organizations—including corporate, educational, religious, and government groups—are sponsoring volunteer programs. In addition, more and more people are volunteering in a wide range of ways. People volunteer for many different reasons: some for political or religious reasons; some for personal or social reasons. Others volunteer simply because it's mandatory, or required, in certain situations; for example, as part of a school's curriculum.

---

[1] *bestows:* gives to

Read what the following people say about volunteering. Why do you think they donate, or give, their time? Match the people with their reasons for volunteering. Some people may have more than one reason. Share your answers in a small group.

Reasons for volunteering		
personal	medical research	mandatory
political	religious	environmental

1. Ralph Birdsong, age 42
   Raised $2,000 for AIDS research in the annual Boston-to-New York AIDS bicycle ride

   "First of all, I'm trying to raise money for AIDS research in memory of my brother. Maybe this way what happened to him won't happen to others. Second, I enjoy biking and this way I can combine my hobby with a good cause."

   Reasons: *personal and medical research* _____

2. Greg Dean, age 36
   Donates his time as a Boy Scout leader

   "I've always loved the outdoors and camping. By being a Scout leader, I can do something I like and transmit my love of nature to another generation. Maybe they'll take care of it better than our generation has."

   Reasons: _____

3. Ellen Bullard, age 27
   Volunteers in a soup kitchen for the homeless

   "I've always been taught that we should help those who are less fortunate than we are. When Reverend Kingsford spoke at church last Sunday about all the good work being done here, I just knew I wanted to participate."

   Reasons: _____

4. Jake Hutchings, age 17
   Spends three hours a week playing guitar for senior citizens in a nursing home

   "I started working here last year because it was a school requirement. This year it's an extracurricular activity. I asked the director of the program if I could come back again this year because I really have a good time with these people. I think they like to listen to my music, too."

   Reasons: _____

5. Marcia Pantani, age 58
   Spends five hours a week volunteering at a politician's headquarters

   "I feel that this person is the best candidate. By volunteering for her, I can do more than just vote. I feel like I'm more involved in the whole political process."

   Reasons: _____

VOCABULARY FOR COMPREHENSION

1 *Reading One is about a boy who uses his love of bicycles to help people in need. Match the words on the left with the different parts of the bicycle.*

a. seat

b. frame

c. pedal

d. spoke

e. brakes

f. wheel

g. grips

h. tire

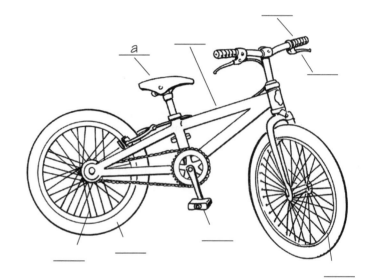

2 *Work with a partner. Two of the three words in each row are similar in meaning to the boldfaced word. Cross out the word that does not belong. If you need help, use a dictionary.*

1. **judgment**	decision	~~offer~~	opinion
2. **proud**	modest	pleased	content
3. **challenge**	allow	test	demand
4. **satisfaction**	happiness	pleasure	amusement
5. **determined**	insistent	stubborn	uncertain

6. proposal	suggestion	order	recommendation
7. donate	contribute	give	sell
8. admire	respect	regard	accept
9. devote	dedicate	take	give
10. inspire	lessen	encourage	motivate
11. battered	broken	hurt	complete
12. thrilled	happy	saddened	excited

2 Focus on Reading

A   READING ONE: *Justin Lebo*

Justin Lebo is a young boy who volunteers his time and energy to help others in a unique way. Read the first two paragraphs and answer the following questions with a partner. Then read the rest of the article.

1. What condition is the bicycle in?

2. Why do you think Justin says the bicycle is "perfect"?

3. What do you think Justin will do with the bicycle?

JUSTIN LEBO

BY PHILLIP HOOSE
(from *It's Our World, Too*)

1   Something about the battered old bicycle at the garage sale[1] caught ten-year-old Justin Lebo's eye. What a wreck! It was like looking at a few big bones in the dust and trying to figure out what kind of dinosaur they had once belonged to.

2   It was a BMX bike with a twenty-inch frame. Its original color was buried beneath five or six coats of gunky paint. Everything—the grips, the pedals, the brakes, the seat, the spokes—was bent or broken, twisted and rusted. Justin stood back as if he were inspecting a painting for sale at an auction. Then he made his final judgment: perfect.

[1] *garage sale:* a sale of used furniture, clothes, toys, etc. held at someone's home, usually in someone's garage

3   Justin talked the owner down to $6.50 and asked his mother, Diane, to help load the bike into the back of their car.

4   When he got it home, he wheeled the junker into the garage and showed it proudly to his father. "Will you help me fix it up?" he asked. Justin's hobby was bike racing, a passion the two of them shared. Their garage barely had room for the car anymore. It was more like a bike shop. Tires and frames hung from hooks on the ceiling, and bike wrenches dangled from the walls.

5   Now Justin and his father cleared out a work space in the garage and put the old junker up on a rack. They poured alcohol on the frame and rubbed until the old paint began to yield, layer by layer. They replaced the broken pedal, tightened down a new seat, and restored the grips. In about a week, it looked brand new.

6   Soon he forgot about the bike. But the very next week, he bought another junker at a yard sale[2] and fixed it up, too. After a while it both-ered him that he wasn't really using either bike. Then he realized that what he loved about the old bikes wasn't riding them: it was the challenge of making something new and useful out of something old and broken.

7   Justin wondered what he should do with them. They were just taking up space in the garage. He remembered that when he was younger, he used to live near a large brick building called the Kilbarchan Home for Boys. It was a place for boys whose parents couldn't care for them for one reason or another.

8   He found "Kilbarchan" in the phone book and called the director, who said the boys would be thrilled to get two bicycles. The next day when Justin and his mother unloaded the bikes at the home, two boys raced out to greet them. They leapt aboard the bikes and started tool-ing around the semicircular driveway, doing wheelies and pirouettes, laughing and shouting.

[2] *yard sale:* another phrase for *garage sale*

9   The Lebos watched them for a while, then started to climb into their car to go home. The boys cried after them, "Wait a minute! You forgot your bikes!" Justin explained that the bikes were for them to keep. "They were so happy." Justin remembers. "It was like they couldn't believe it. It made me feel good just to see them happy."

10   On the way home, Justin was silent. His mother assumed he was lost in a feeling of satisfaction. But he was thinking about what would happen once those bikes got wheeled inside and everybody saw them. How could all those kids decide who got the bikes? Two bikes could cause more trouble than they would solve. Actually they hadn't been that hard to build. It was fun. Maybe he could do more . . .

11   "Mom," Justin said as they turned onto their street, "I've got an idea. I'm going to make a bike for every boy at Kilbarchan for Christmas." Diane Lebo looked at Justin out of the corner of her eye. She had rarely seen him so determined.

12   When they got home, Justin called Kilbarchan to find out how many boys lived there. There were twenty-one. It was already June. He had six months to make nineteen bikes. That was almost a bike a week. Justin called the home back to tell them of his plan. "I could tell they didn't think I could do it," Justin remembers. "I knew I could."

13   Justin knew his best chance to build bikes was almost the way General Motors or Ford builds cars: in an assembly line. He figured it would take three or four junkers to produce enough parts to make one good bike. That meant sixty to eighty bikes. Where would he get them?

14   Garage sales seemed to be the only hope. It was June, and there would be garage sales all summer long. But even if he could find that many bikes, how could he ever pay for them? That was hundreds of dollars.

15   He went to his parents with a proposal. "When Justin was younger, say five or six," says his mother, "he used to give away some of his allowance[3] to help others in need. His father and I would donate a dollar for every dollar Justin donated. So he asked us if it could be like the old days, if we'd match every dollar he put into buying old bikes. We said yes."

16   Justin and his mother spent most of June and July hunting for cheap bikes at garage sales and thrift shops.[4] They would haul the bikes home, and Justin would start stripping them down in the yard.

17   But by the beginning of August, he had managed to make only ten bikes. Summer vacation was almost over, and school and homework would soon cut into his time. Garage sales would dry up when it got colder, and Justin was out of money. Still he was determined to find a way.

18   At the end of August, Justin got a break. A neighbor wrote a letter to the local newspaper describing Justin's project, and an editor thought it would make a good story. In her admiring article about a boy who was devoting his summer to help kids he didn't even know, she said Justin needed bikes and money, and she printed his home phone number.

---

[3] *allowance:* money that you are given regularly or for a special reason
[4] *thrift shops:* stores that sell used furniture, clothes, toys, etc., at a low price

19   Overnight, everything changed. "There must have been a hundred calls," Justin says. "People would call me up and ask me to come over and pick up their old bike. Or I'd be working in the garage, and a station wagon would pull up. The driver would leave a couple of bikes by the curb. It just snowballed."

20   The week before Christmas Justin delivered the last of the twenty-one bikes to Kilbarchan. Once again, the boys poured out of the home and leapt aboard the bikes, tearing around in the snow.

21   And once again, their joy inspired Justin. They reminded him how important bikes were to him. Wheels meant freedom. He thought about how much more the freedom to ride must mean to boys like these who had so little freedom in their lives. He decided to keep on building.

22   "First I made eleven bikes for the children in a foster home⁵ my mother told me about. Then I made bikes for all the women in a battered women's shelter. Then I made ten little bikes and tricycles for children with AIDS. Then I made twenty-three bikes for the Paterson Housing Coalition."

23   In the four years since he started, Justin Lebo has made between 150 and 200 bikes and given them all away. He has been careful to leave time for his homework, his friends, his coin collection, his new interest in marine biology, and of course, his own bikes.

24   Reporters and interviewers have asked Justin Lebo the same question over and over: "Why do you do it?" The question seems to make him uncomfortable. It's as if they want him to say what a great person he is. Their stories always make him seem like a saint, which he knows he isn't. "Sure it's nice of me to make the bikes," he says, "because I don't have to. But I want to. In part, I do it for myself. I don't think you can ever really do anything to help anybody else if it doesn't make you happy."

25   "Once I overheard a kid who got one of my bikes say, 'A bike is like a book; it opens up a whole new world.' That's how I feel, too. It made me happy to know that kid felt that way. That's why I do it."

---

⁵ *foster home:* a temporary home where a child is taken care of by someone who is not a parent or legal guardian

READING FOR MAIN IDEAS

Complete the following statements. Share your answers with a partner.

1. Justin Lebo is a _____

_____

_____ .

2. Justin is a special person because _____

_____

_____ .

3. His parents and the community have supported him by _____

_____

_____ .

4. Justin enjoys doing what he does because _____

_____

_____ .

READING FOR DETAILS

This chart lists some benefits of doing community service. Complete the chart with examples of how Justin Lebo benefited from his experience.

THE BENEFITS OF COMMUNITY SERVICE	EXAMPLE OF JUSTIN LEBO
Encourages people to use their free time constructively	Justin spent his free time in the summer making bicycles for the children at the Kilbarchan Home for Boys.
Gives a sense of satisfaction and builds self-esteem	
Opens people's eyes to the great variety of people in need	
One successful community service experience leads to performing other services	
Helps people to find out who they are, what their interests are, and what they are good at	

REACTING TO THE READING

1 *Read the following questions and circle the letter of the best answer. If necessary, refer back to the reading to support your answer. When you are finished, compare answers with a partner.*

1. Which of the following statements best describes Justin's reaction to the first bike he saw at the garage sale?
   a. He knew immediately that the bike could be fixed up and used by someone who needed a bike.
   b. He wasn't exactly sure what he would do with the bike after he fixed it up, but he was sure he would think of something.
   c. He only knew he wanted to fix up the bike.

2. Which of the following statements best describes why Justin enjoyed fixing the first two bikes?
   a. He liked riding them.
   b. He liked taking them apart and putting them back together.
   c. He liked saving the bikes from being thrown away and making them useful again.

3. Which of the following statements best describes what Justin was thinking about on his way home from the Kilbarchan Home for Boys?
   a. He knew he had to fix up enough bikes for all the children.
   b. He was satisfied with his work and felt very proud of himself.
   c. He was happy that the boys enjoyed the bikes so much.

4. Which of the following statements best describes the director of the Kilbarchan Home's reaction to Justin's plan of making each boy a bicycle?
   a. He was pleased and knew Justin had the determination to complete his plan.
   b. He thought that Justin was an incredibly generous child.
   c. He was surprised and didn't really believe Justin could do it.

5. Which of the following helped Justin most with his bike acquisitions?
   a. His parents' agreement to help him with money.
   b. The newspaper article written about his project.
   c. The fact that it was summer and there were many yard sales.

6. Which of the following statements best describes Justin's motivation for continuing to build and give away bikes?
   a. He loves bicycles and wants other people to have the opportunity to see how wonderful they are.
   b. He loves the challenge of repairing and restoring bicycles that would otherwise be thrown away.
   c. He loves the satisfaction of doing things for other people.

7. Which of the following statements best describes Justin Lebo?
   a. He is a young man with a wide range of interests and hobbies.
   b. He is a young man whose interests are centered on bike racing and repair.
   c. He is a young man who is continually changing his interests and hobbies.

8. Which of the following reasons describes why Justin Lebo does what he does?
   a. His parents have encouraged him to help others.
   b. It makes him happy to help others.
   c. Helping others is mandatory at his school.

2 *Choose one of the following quotations from Sharing Information on page 112 and write a short paragraph explaining how it applies to Justin Lebo and his bicycle project.*

"It is better to give than to receive."
—Acts 20:35, Bible, Revised Standard Version

"A person's true wealth is the good he or she does in the world."
—Mohammed

"He who bestows his goods upon the poor,
Shall have as much again, and ten times more."
—John Bunyan, *Pilgrim's Progress,* Part Two, Section VII

B   READING TWO: *Some Take the Time Gladly / Mandatory Volunteering*

Many educational organizations in the United States believe that a high school graduation requirement should be that students devote a certain number of hours outside of the classroom to community service. Supporters of mandatory volunteering believe that the school's role should include not only preparing children to be academically successful, but also helping them to be responsible citizens and active participants in their communities.

However, not everybody believes that mandatory volunteering is a good idea. Those opposed to the requirement believe that the term "mandatory volunteering" is an oxymoron, a contradiction; they believe that volunteering should be something you do of your own free will. It is not something that is forced on you.

Do you believe mandatory volunteering is a good idea? Why or why not?

Some Take the Time Gladly

By Mensah Dean (from the *Washington Times*)

1   Mandatory volunteering made many members of Maryland's high school class of '97 grumble with indignation.

2   Future seniors,[1] however, probably won't be as resistant now that the program has been broken in. Some, like John Maloney, already have completed their required hours of approved community service. The Bowie High School sophomore[2] earned his hours in eighth grade[3] by volunteering two nights a week at the Larkin-Chase Nursing and Restorative Center in Bowie.

3   He played shuffleboard, cards, and other games with the senior citizens.[4] He also helped plan parties for them and visited their rooms to keep them company.

4   John, fifteen, is not finished volunteering. Once a week he videotapes animals at the Prince George County animal shelter in Forestville. His footage is shown on the Bowie public access television channel in hopes of finding homes for the animals.

5   "Volunteering is better than just sitting around," says John, "and I like animals; I don't want to see them put to sleep."[5]

6   He's not the only volunteer in his family. His sister, Melissa, an eighth grader, has completed her hours also volunteering at Larkin-Chase.

7   "It is a good idea to have kids go out into the community, but it's frustrating to have to write essays about the work," she said. "It makes you feel like you're doing it for the requirement and not for yourself."

8   The high school's service learning office, run by Beth Ansley, provides information on organizations seeking volunteers so that students will have an easier time fulfilling their hours.

9   "It's ridiculous that people are opposing the requirements," said Amy Rouse, who this summer has worked at the Ronald McDonald House[6] and has helped to rebuild a church in Clinton.

10   "So many people won't do the service unless it's mandatory," Rouse said, "but once they start doing it, they'll really like it and hopefully it will become a part of their lives—like it has become a part of mine."

---

[1] *seniors:* students in the last year of high school, approximately 17–18 years old
[2] *sophomore:* a student in the second year of high school, approximately 15–16 years old
[3] *eighth grade:* The U.S. public school system begins with kindergarten and then continues with grades 1–12. A student in eighth grade is approximately 13–14 years old.
[4] *senior citizens:* people 65 years old and older
[5] *put to sleep:* to give an animal drugs so that it dies without pain
[6] *Ronald McDonald House:* a residence, usually near a hospital, which provides a home and other support services for the family of children who require a lot of time in the hospital because of serious illness

Mandatory Volunteering for High School Diploma Not a Good Idea

(from the *Sun Sentinel*)

1   Re: proposals for mandatory service hours in order to graduate from high school: I am an active participant in the high school service program, and chairperson of a tutoring program run primarily by high school students such as myself. Volunteering is a personal choice and an extracurricular activity such as the debate team or school-sponsored sports.

2   Mandatory volunteering is not a good idea. First, many students do volunteer, and most do it with full force. By the time a volunteering student becomes a senior, that student could earn as many as 1000+ service hours. If an entering freshman[1] is told that he or she must volunteer for a pre-set number of hours, the student might become resentful, complete the required hours, and never volunteer again. The volunteered hours would end up being less than the hours being volunteered now.

3   Many students do not have the time to volunteer. School goes from a set starting time to a set ending time. If the student's busy after-school schedule does not allow for extracurricular[2] activities, that is the student's own business. With the exception of homework, there is nothing that a student is required to do after school hours.

4   Finally, mandatory volunteering is an oxymoron. If students are required to volunteer, it is no longer volunteering. The performed service becomes one more thing to do in order to graduate from high school. The quality of work can suffer greatly. If a student enjoys volunteering, he or she will volunteer without having to be told.

[1] *freshman:* a student in the first year of high school, approximately 14–15 years old
[2] *extracurricular:* outside of the school requirement

List the reasons for the opinions in the editorials. Share your list with the class.

FOR MANDATORY VOLUNTEERING	AGAINST MANDATORY VOLUNTEERING

C LINKING READINGS ONE AND TWO

Imagine you are Justin Lebo. Write a letter to one of the two people from the editorials in Reading Two. Use your own experience as a volunteer to either disagree with or support the position stated in the editorials and explain why.

Justin Lebo

Dear _____:

    I would like to express my thoughts on your recent editorial on mandatory volunteering.

_____

_____

_____

_____

_____

_____

_____

_____

_____

_____

_____

_____

_____

_____

                                   Sincerely,

                                   Justin Lebo

3 Focus on Vocabulary

1 *Complete the chart with the forms of the words found in the readings. Not all of the words have four forms. If you need help, use a dictionary.*

NOUN	VERB	ADJECTIVE	ADVERB
admiration	*admire*	admiring	*admiringly*
	devote		
challenge			X
	determine		X
	donate	X	X
		fulfilling	X
hope			
	X	indignant	
	inspire		
	manage		X
	oppose		X
passion	X		
proposal			X
	X	proud	
		ridiculous	
snowball		X	X
		thrilled	X
volunteer			

Complete the sentences on page 126. For verbs, use the correct tense and check subject-verb agreement.

1. Justin Lebo had to rely on _____ from people in order to
(donate)

complete the bicycles for the children at Kilbarchin.

2. Justin felt _____ when he saw how the boys enjoyed the first
(inspire)

two bicycles he had made.

3. Many people hope that after experiencing mandatory volunteering, students

will become _____ about volunteering in general.
(passion)

4. Justin Lebo met the _____ of making a bike for each boy at
(challenge)

Kilbarchin.

5. When Justin _____ that his parents give a dollar for every
(proposal)

dollar he donated, they agreed.

6. Justin's parents wanted to help him, but they were not really

_____ that he could succeed in making a bike for every
(hope)

boy at Kilbarchin.

7. Although many people support mandatory volunteering, there is still a lot

of _____ to it.
(oppose)

2 *A phrasal verb consists of a verb and a particle. This combination of words often has a meaning that is different from the meaning of its separate parts. Work in a small group. Read the following sentences. Circle the letter of the best explanation for each underlined phrasal verb.*

1. Proponents of mandatory volunteering say volunteering for community
service is time better spent than <u>sitting around</u> all day watching television or
playing computer games.
   a. doing nothing special
   b. sitting with friends in a circle
   c. not taking part in something

2. Little boys and girls love to <u>tear around</u> on bicycles that Justin Lebo made.
   a. play so hard you rip your clothes
   b. move quickly in all directions
   c. destroy things

3. Students who have lots of free time like to <u>tool around</u> town on bikes or in cars.
   a. play with hammers, screwdrivers, and other tools
   b. terrorize a place in or on a vehicle
   c. take a ride in or on a vehicle

4. At first, Justin could not <u>figure out</u> what to do with his two bikes.
   a. resolve a problem
   b. make a plan
   c. take part in

5. Justin had so many bikes that he had to <u>clear out</u> his basement and start building them there.
   a. make room on a table
   b. clean an area or space
   c. empty an area or space

6. When the students <u>found out</u> the new graduation requirements, they were furious.
   a. created something
   b. discovered something lost
   c. learned a new fact or information about something

7. Justin Lebo <u>talked</u> the bicycle owner <u>down</u> $3.00.
   a. discussed a situation
   b. spoke disrespectfully to someone
   c. persuaded someone to reduce a price

8. People fear that if students do not do community service, they will <u>end up</u> being uncaring and unsympathetic individuals.
   a. complete a project
   b. finish in a certain way
   c. stop something

9. When people donate old clothes to a community center, the center staff will often come to the house and <u>pick up</u> the donations.
   a. start to increase
   b. clean something
   c. collect something

10. Justin was afraid that the garage sales would <u>dry up</u> by the end of the summer.
    a. be dull and uninteresting
    b. slowly come to an end
    c. become useless

3 *How do you think these people would answer the questions? Read the question and write their answer, using the words given. Change the word form or tense if necessary. Share your responses with a partner.*

1. To Diane Lebo:
   Your son Justin is quite remarkable, isn't he?

   devote   **determine**   **proud**   **tear around**

   Yes, he is. After Justin saw the boys tearing around on their bicycles, he

   became devoted to the project. He was determined to get every boy on a

   bicycle and he did. I'm very proud of him.

2. To Justin Lebo:
   After fixing the first bike, did you ever think you would end up repairing and donating over 150 more?

   passion   **challenge**   **snowball**   **sit around**

   _____

   _____

   _____

3. To the director of the Kilbarchan School for Boys:
   What did you think when Justin first told you he was planning on building a bicycle for every boy at Kilbarchan?

   thrilled   **proposal**   **manage**   **end up**

   _____

   _____

   _____

4. To a Kilbarchan boy:
   How did you feel when you rode one of Justin's bikes?

   hope   **inspire**   **admire**   **tool around**

   _____

   _____

   _____

5. To a student who supports mandatory volunteering:
   Why do you support mandatory volunteering?

   fulfilling   **donate**   **volunteer**   **figure out**

   _____

   _____

   _____

6. To a student who opposes mandatory volunteering:
   Why are you opposed to mandatory volunteering?

   ridiculous   **indignant**   **oppose**   **find out**

   _____

   _____

   _____

4 Focus on Writing

A GRAMMAR: Tag Questions

1 *Examine the following sentences. Then discuss the questions with a partner.*

   a. Justin Lebo is a philanthropist, <u>isn't he</u>?

   b. Justin Lebo doesn't sell his bikes, <u>does he</u>?

   c. He and his father fixed bikes, <u>didn't they</u>?

   1. There are two parts to a tag question. What are they?

   2. What are the tags in these questions?

   3. When the verb in the statement is affirmative, what is the verb in the tag part? What happens to the tag when the verb in the statement is negative?

Tag Questions

Tag questions consist of a statement and a tag. Tags are questions that are added on to the end of the statement. Tag questions are like *yes/no* questions. They are often used to check information or ask for agreement. They usually mean, "Isn't the statement I've just made true? Aren't I right?" Tag questions are answered in the same way as *yes/no* questions.

He is a philanthropist, **isn't he**? **Yes,** he is./**No,** he isn't.

(continued)

Affirmative and Negative Forms

Tag questions are made up of two parts: a statement and the tag.

If the verb in the statement is affirmative, the verb in the tag is negative. The negative verb in the tag is always a contraction.

Justin **is** young, **isn't** he?

If the verb in the statement is negative, the verb in the tag is affirmative.

Justin **isn't** old, **is** he?

Subject Agreement

The subject of the tag agrees with the subject of the statement. The subject in the tag is always a subject pronoun.

Mandatory volunteering is ridiculous, isn't **it**?

Many students are volunteers, aren't **they**?

Justin doesn't have to volunteer, does **he**?

Verb Agreement

The verb in the tag is the same tense as the verb in the statement and agrees with the statement verb in number and person. The verb in the tag is always a form of *be* or an auxiliary verb.

Statement	Tag
1. be (main verb) Volunteering **wasn't** a requirement,	**was** it?
2. be (auxiliary verb) You **were** going to volunteer last week,	**weren't** you?
3. have (auxiliary verb) Justin **has** fixed more than 200 bikes,	**hasn't** he?

4. modal (auxiliary verb)
     You **will** help us with the project,
     They **can't** graduate until they volunteer,
	won't you?
	can they?

5. other verbs (main verb) Justin's father **helped** him fix up the bikes,	**didn't** he?
6. have (main verb) You **have** some free time to volunteer,	**don't** you?

2 *Match the following statements with the correct tags.*

1. Private donations helped establish churches, hospitals, libraries, and universities, __f__

2. Nearly all civilizations have practiced some form of philanthropy, _____

3. Many corporations give money to support the arts, _____

4. Volunteering in senior citizen centers can really make a difference, _____

5. Some people haven't reacted well to the idea of forcing community service, _____

6. Mandatory volunteering is an oxymoron, _____

7. You won't forget to take food to the homeless shelter, _____

8. Mandatory volunteering isn't a good idea, _____

9. Students shouldn't have to do mandatory volunteering, _____

10. You are proud of yourself when you volunteer, _____

11. You would like to do something like Justin is doing, _____

12. By Christmas, she had baked over 1,000 cookies for children in foster care, _____

a. isn't it?	g. wouldn't you?
b. will you?	h. can't it?
c. should they?	i. hadn't she?
d. don't they?	j. have they?
e. is it?	k. aren't you?
f. didn't they?	l. haven't they?

3 *Some of the following tag questions have grammatical errors. Find the errors and make the corrections. Not all the sentences have errors.*

                                                             didn't

1. Justin Lebo fixed up three bicycles yesterday, ~~doesn't~~ he?

2. John is not finished volunteering, is John?

3. Corporations have been donating more and more to the needy, haven't they?

4. It's ridiculous for people to oppose the requirements, is not it?

5. Students shouldn't be forced to do volunteer work, shouldn't they?

6. Students who volunteer will be more likely to attend four-year colleges, won't they?

7. Students who volunteer in high school will continue to volunteer throughout their lives, aren't they?

8. People's reaction to mandatory volunteering is mixed, isn't it?

9. The bikes weren't that hard to build, didn't they?

10. Justin used to give away some of his allowance to help others in need, didn't he?

B   STYLE: Punctuation

1 *Examine these sentences. Pay close attention to the punctuation. With a partner, discuss the questions that follow.*

    a. Justin didn't have to volunteer, did he?

    b. I like animals; I don't want to see them put to sleep.

    c. Justin stood back as if he were inspecting a painting for sale at an auction and then made his final judgment: perfect.

    d. Everything—the grips, the pedals, the brakes, the seat, the spokes—was bent or broken, twisted and rusted.

1. In which sentence does the punctuation set off a list of extra information? _____

2. In which sentence does the punctuation separate two closely related statements? _____

3. In which sentence does the punctuation set off a word which identifies and clarifies other words that come before it? _____

4. In which sentence does the punctuation set off a question? _____

Punctuation

The Comma (,)

Use a comma to

- connect a dependent clause to an independent clause when the dependent clause starts the sentence.

- separate items in a list of three or more elements that match in grammatical form.

- coordinate independent clauses.

- introduce a quotation.

- separate the tag from the statement when forming a tag question.

Examples

If Justin hadn't been interested in bicycles, he might have found another way to help others.

Justin has been careful to leave time for his homework, his friends, his coin collection, his new interest in marine biology, and of course his own bikes.

Justin had already donated two bikes, but he still wasn't done.

The boys cried after them, "Wait a minute!"

Mandatory volunteering isn't accepted by everyone, is it?

The Semicolon (;)

Use a semicolon to

- connect two independent clauses with very closely related ideas.

Example

A bike is like a book; it opens up a whole new world.

The Colon (:)

Use a colon to

- illustrate or give further information about a noun or noun phrase.

- introduce a quotation. This is a more formal way to introduce quotations than the use of a comma (,).

Examples

Justin knew his best chance to build bikes was almost the way General Motors or Ford builds cars: in an assembly line.

Reporters and interviewers have asked Justin Lebo the same question over and over: "Why do you do it?"

(continued)

The Dash (—)	Examples
Use a dash to	
• set off extra information, especially if the information has a series of commas.	Everything—the grips, the pedals, the brakes—was broken.
• indicate parenthetical information or a sudden break in thought.	Volunteering for community service—whether it be mandatory or not—is a great way to get students involved in society.
• emphasize or summarize a thought.	Hopefully, it will become a part of their lives—as it has become a part of mine.

2 *Look at the following pairs of sentences. Circle the letter of the sentence in each pair that correctly uses commas, colons, semicolons, and dashes. Review the explanations in the chart, and explain the use of punctuation in each sentence.*

1. (a.) Justin stood back as if he were inspecting a painting for sale at an auction. Then he made his final judgment: perfect.

   b. Justin stood back as if he were inspecting a painting for sale at an auction. Then he made his final judgment—perfect.

   The colon is used to give further information about a noun or noun phrase.

2. a. Many schools are starting to make mandatory volunteering a graduation requirement; aren't they?

   b. Many schools are starting to make mandatory volunteering a graduation requirement, aren't they?

   _____

3. a. All of Lev's work—which is a lot—has been focused on the homeless.

   b. All of Lev's work: which is a lot, has been focused on the homeless.

   _____

4. a. In order to fix the bicycles, Justin Lebo needed to have lots of spare parts; chains, pedals, seats, and cables.

   b. In order to fix the bicycles, Justin Lebo needed to have lots of spare parts: chains, pedals, seats, and cables.

   _____

5. a. There are many types of community service—working in soup kitchens, working in nursing homes, working at homeless shelters—which high school students can choose to do.

   b. There are many types of community service; working in soup kitchens, working in nursing homes, working at homeless shelters; which high school students can choose to do.

---

6. a. Although many people consider "mandatory volunteering" an oxymoron, that doesn't mean it isn't a good idea.

   b. Although many people consider "mandatory volunteering" an oxymoron: that doesn't mean it isn't a good idea.

---

7. a. Most volunteers at some time ask themselves the same question—"Why is it important for me to do this?"

   b. Most volunteers at some time ask themselves the same question: "Why is it important for me to do this?"

---

8. a. Volunteering is becoming more and more important in the college application process, many colleges look more favorably on students who have volunteered in high school.

   b. Volunteering is becoming more and more important in the college application process; many colleges look more favorably on students who have volunteered in high school.

---

9. a. Justin donated bikes to the Kilbarchin Home for Boys, the Paterson Housing Coalition, and a battered women's shelter.

   b. Justin donated bikes to the Kilbarchin Home for Boys—the Paterson Housing Coalition—and a battered women's shelter.

---

3 *Add the correct punctuation to this paragraph. Use a comma (,), colon (:), semicolon (;), or dash (—). In one case, there are two correct answers.*

I began volunteering at the age of 14. At the time, there was no mandatory volunteering requirement (**1**) __:__ volunteering was a personal choice based on my own interest. My interests centered on helping children (**2**) _____ especially children with special needs. At our school, we had a special needs classroom with a number of special needs children. Twice a week, I would work as the teacher's helper. Through the work I did, I realized two things (**3**) _____ I was happiest when I volunteered, and I was good at helping special needs students. I am now much older (**4**) _____ have a college degree in special education, and still do volunteer work at a community center for troubled teenagers. I guess I would say that the volunteer work I did at age 14 changed my life (**5**) _____ forever.

C WRITING TOPICS

Write an essay about one of these topics. Be sure to use some of the ideas, vocabulary, grammar, and style that you have learned in this unit.

1. Imagine you are responsible for setting up a community service program in your city. What kind of program would you start? Who would it serve? Would there be volunteers? Who would the volunteers be? What would you hope to accomplish? Be as specific as possible.

2. In your opinion, what are the pros and cons of mandatory volunteering in high school? Describe both sides of the issue.

3. Many large corporations are involved in philanthropic work. They often say that they want to give something back to the people and community that have supported them and their products. Their money and efforts do a lot of good; however, some people might say that they are really just looking for a "tax break" or a cheap way to buy good publicity for the company. What is your opinion on corporate philanthropy? Give examples to support your opinion.

4. Look at the quotation from John Bunyan on page 112. There are many different ways to "bestow your goods upon the poor." Write about some of these ways and why you think people perform these acts.

D RESEARCH TOPIC

Report on a center or project in your community.

Step 1: As a class, brainstorm a list of community centers or community work being done in your area, or list types of community centers you have heard about. Discuss the types of services these centers offer: serving food, offering shelter, meeting medical or educational needs, helping repair homes, cleaning up the neighborhood, or others.

Step 2: Work in a small group. Research one of the centers or community projects. Individually, or in groups, go to a center or project headquarters and gather information to complete the chart below. If there is not a center or project near you, go to the library or online and find information about activities in another area.

Step 3: Combine your information and write a report and present it to the class. Use the chart to organize your report.

Name of center or project	
History: When was it started? Who started it? Why?	
Type of people helped	
Type of people who work there: Are there volunteers? How many? Who are they?	
Funding: How are activities paid for? Where does the funding come from?	

For step-by-step practice in the writing process, see the *Writing Activity Book, High Intermediate,* Unit 6.

Assignment	Persuasive essay
Prewriting	Listing pros and cons
Organizing	Persuading the reader
Revising	Writing an effective introduction and conclusion
	Using tag questions to involve the reader
Editing	Using semicolons, colons, and dashes

For Unit 6 Internet activities, visit the NorthStar Companion Website at
http://www.longman.com/northstar

Homing in on Education

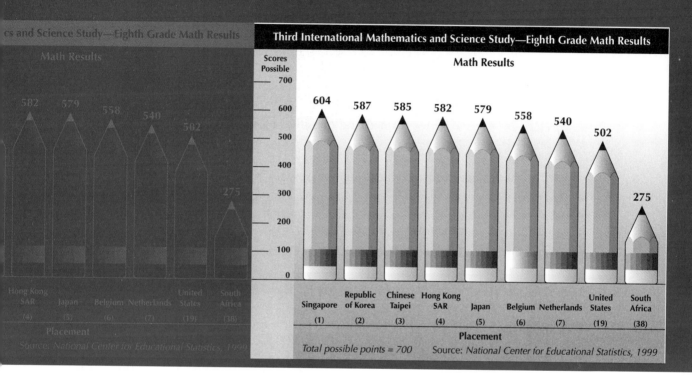

Singapore	Republic of Korea	Chinese Taipei	Hong Kong SAR	Japan	Belgium	Netherlands	United States	South Africa
(1)	(2)	(3)	(4)	(5)	(6)	(7)	(19)	(38)

Third International Mathematics and Science Study—Eighth Grade Math Results

Math Results

Total possible points = 700   Source: *National Center for Educational Statistics, 1999*

1 Focus on the Topic

A PREDICTING

Look at the graph. It shows test scores from an International Mathematics and Science Study. The math test was given to eighth-grade[1] students in 38 countries. The test compared academic performance among the participating countries. The graph shows the ranks and scores of nine countries. Work in a small group. Discuss these questions.

1. What countries are among the top seven? Where did the United States place?

2. What are your reactions to the test results?

3. Why do you think the students from the top countries scored well?

---

[1] Eighth-grade students are approximately 13–14 years old.

B   SHARING INFORMATION

According to research, three of the factors listed below contribute to a student's success. Check (✓) each factor you believe contributed to the success of the top-scoring countries in the International Mathematics and Science Study. Discuss your opinions with the class. Then compare your opinions with the answers at the bottom of the page.

Students in the top scoring countries:

_____ **1.** spend more time on homework.

_____ **2.** spend less time watching television.

_____ **3.** have easy access to computers and books in the home.

_____ **4.** have better trained and qualified teachers.

_____ **5.** spend more time in class.

_____ **6.** have more challenging coursework (curricula).

_____ **7.** spend less time playing with friends after school.

_____ **8.** have smaller class sizes.

C   PREPARING TO READ

BACKGROUND

The term *home schooling* or *home tuition,* as it is called in England, means educating children at home or in places other than a <u>mainstream</u> setting, such as a public or private school. There are many reasons why parents choose home schooling for their children. Some parents are dissatisfied with the quality of education in the public schools. Others do not want their children to have to worry about <u>peer pressure</u>. They say it may interfere with the child's studies and can also lead to negative behavior such as smoking, drinking alcohol, and taking drugs. <u>Bullying</u> and harassing from other students is another concern. Still other parents choose this type of education for religious reasons. Whatever the reasons may be, it is evident that more and more children are being taken out of mainstream schools every year. As a result, many questions have <u>emerged</u>, encouraging the debate over home schooling versus traditional forms of schooling.

What then is the future of education? Will this <u>marginal</u> model of schooling replace traditional schools and conventional methods? Will computers and the Internet replace our classrooms and teachers? Will traditional schools be a <u>thing of the past</u>? As the debate over home schooling versus traditional schooling continues, so do the questions about what home schoolers are studying at home. How can parents <u>ensure</u> that their children are prepared academically for college? How are home schoolers <u>assessed</u> to make sure they are getting the

Answers: 3, 4, and 6.

basics—the same educational standards that mainstream students must have? Finally, there are questions regarding the children's emotional development. Are home schoolers <u>isolated</u> from their peers? Are they <u>missing out</u> on the social benefits of being in a large classroom of their peers? As with any <u>debatable</u> issue, the answers to these questions are neither simple nor one-sided.

Complete these sentences.

1. The four main reasons for home schooling are:

    a. _____

    b. _____

    c. _____

    d. _____

2. Some people have concerns about home schooling. Four of these concerns are:

    a. _____

    b. _____

    c. _____

    d. _____

3. I might (or I might not) teach a child at home because _____

    _____

VOCABULARY FOR COMPREHENSION

Find the underlined words in the reading on pages 140–141. Write each word beside its synonym below.

_____*debatable*_____ **a.** controversial, questionable

_____ **b.** developed, arisen

_____ **c.** guarantee

_____ **d.** losing an opportunity for

_____ **e.** not typical

_____ **f.** separated or secluded from

_____ **g.** social demands from your "group"

_____ **h.** something that is not used anymore or is obsolete

_____ **i.** tested, evaluated

_____ **j.** threatening, teasing

_____ **k.** traditional, conventional

2 Focus on Reading

Read the title of the article and the first paragraph. Write three questions which you would like the article to answer. Use the question words given. Then read the rest of the article.

1. Where _____ ?

2. How _____ ?

3. Why _____ ?

Teaching at Home Hits New High with Internet
As Schools Fight for a Future, 15,000 Families Join the Trend Towards Teaching Children at Home

By Dorothy Lepkowska (from the *Evening Standard*)

1   Record numbers of children are being taken out of school and educated by their parents at home. Up to 100 children a month nationally are leaving the classroom because of their parents' disillusionment with the education system. Around 15,000 families are now teaching their youngsters at home, a rise of 50 percent from last year, according to latest figures.

2   The popularity of home tuition [home schooling] has traditionally been blamed on the rigidity of the examination system, parents being unable to get their children into the school of their choice, and dissatisfaction with teaching methods. Some parents also prefer to keep their children at home because of bullying and a lack of discipline in schools. Academics now claim, however, that a significant proportion of families educating at home do so because they feel that the concept of institution-alised education is a thing of the past. They believe that schools could be obsolete within 20 years as parents turn instead to media technology, such as the Internet, to educate their children.

This article was published in 1996.

3   Under the law, parents must ensure their children are educated, whether at school or at home. It is the responsibility of local authorities to safeguard their schooling. Professor Roland Meighan, a senior lecturer in education at Nottingham University, said parents were fed up with the constrictions of the existing education system. He said: "Schools have become an outdated concept from the days of the town crier,[1] when information was scarce and a central figure was needed to impart knowledge. Parents are now coming to the conclusion that education is moving on, and they do not want their children to be stifled[2] by conventional methods."

4   Professor Meighan said many academics now thought schools as we know them could become obsolete within 20 years. Instead, children will be taught at home using the Internet, computers, and video. He said: "The schools of the future will be small pockets of children, sharing equipment in each others' homes, with teachers taking on a new role as advisers, sorting through the available information."

5   The future of institutionalised schooling was recently called into question by Sir Christopher Ball, the director of learning at the Royal Society of Arts. He predicted the education system of the future would include a global curriculum and a worldwide qualifications[3] system. He said: "Some existing marginal models of schooling will move into the mainstream—community schools and home schooling, for example. No doubt, other models as yet unseen will emerge."

How Opting Out Brings *O-Level* Success at 13

6   Leslie Barson is already running a prototype of the type of school educationalists

predict will educate children in the future. Based partly at a community centre in Brent and partly in family homes, the Otherwise Club is comprised of some 35 families around north London. Professional teachers are brought in where necessary to help with more specialised subjects, but for the most part parents and children work together on projects such as study of the Greeks and the American Civil War, reading up on events, making costumes, and learning how people used to live.

7   Parents opting out of school claim the flexibility of home learning means some children sit one of two GCEs[4] by the age of 13. Ms. Barson's own children, Luis, age 12, and 7-year-old Lilly, have never attended school. She pays around £2,000 a year for private tutors to help in specialised areas. She set up the Otherwise Club six years ago with just a handful of youngsters.

---

[1] *town crier:* in the past, a person employed by a town to make public announcements—usually by shouting in the streets

[2] *stifled:* subdued, restrained

[3] *qualifications:* completion of necessary requirements for graduation

[4] *sit one of two GCEs:* take one of two standardized tests

She said: "The whole idea of educating children should be to develop their self-confidence. Our children do not see adults as disciplinarians." Her son agrees. Luis, who is currently teaching himself math, said: "I like the freedom to learn things that interest me, particularly music. I don't feel I am missing out on anything by not being at school because I am a member of various clubs and have friends who attend normal school."

The "Danger" of Isolating Children

8   Home schooling could affect children's relationships with their peers and other adults because of prolonged periods spent with their parents, educationalists have claimed. Most academics concede that education will in the future be increasingly centred around the home, and fear children could become isolated and withdrawn. Professor Michael Barber, of London University's Institute of Education, said pupils could spend half their time at school and half at home as a compromise. He said home tuition would play an increasingly significant role in educating children in the coming years. "I believe very strongly that children need to have the experience of school," he added. "There is the quality control issue of ensuring pupils are taught the basics and assessed. Children also need to spend time with their peers to learn the rules of work in a democratic society and learn to deal with relationships with adults other than their parents." Margaret Rudland, head teacher of Godolphin and Latymer School, Hammersmith, said children needed to experience the "rough and tumble"[5] of peer associations.

[5] *"rough and tumble"*: hard or demanding aspects

READING FOR MAIN IDEAS

Write whether each sentence is a main idea (MI) or supporting idea (SI).

_MI_   1. Home schooling is increasing in popularity.

_____   2. Around 15,000 families now educate their children at home.

_____   3. Many parents are unhappy with traditional schools.

_____   4. Some educators believe traditional schools will not exist in the future.

_____   5. Some people think the Internet and modern technology will replace the teacher and the classrooms of today.

_____   6. Sir Christopher Ball believes future educational systems will include a worldwide qualifications system.

_____   7. Some people believe isolating home schoolers from their peers can be dangerous.

_____   8. Home schooling may affect children's socialization skills because they spend too much time alone.

READING FOR DETAILS

Circle the letters of the two choices that accurately complete each sentence. Discuss your answers with a partner.

1. It was reported that in England

   a. about 15,000 students have been taken out of school.
   b. no more than 100 children per month are being taken out of school.
   c. more than 100 children per month are being taken out of school.

2. Academics who support home schooling believe

   a. institutionalized education is still important.
   b. schools could be obsolete in 20 years.
   c. media technology and the Internet will become increasingly important in education.

3. Sir Christopher Ball, director of learning at the Royal Society of Arts, predicts that education systems in the future will

   a. have a global curriculum.
   b. include more home schooling and community schools.
   c. have a qualifications system based only on community needs.

4. In the Otherwise Club

   a. students are encouraged to develop self-confidence.
   b. teachers are brought in to teach many of the main subjects.
   c. students attend various clubs and have friends in normal schools.

5. Some educationalists believe home schooling can affect students' relationships with their peers because

   a. the students spend long periods of time with their parents.
   b. the students' lives are centered around their homes.
   c. the students study for many long hours.

REACTING TO THE READING

1 *Complete the chart with information about how the following issues are dealt with in a home school and in a traditional school. If necessary, refer back to the reading for help. When you are finished, discuss your answers with a partner.*

ISSUES	HOME SCHOOL	TRADITIONAL SCHOOL
Peer pressure and bullying	*Students don't have to worry about this because they study at home.*	
Socialization skills		
Teaching methods/ materials		
Role of the teachers		
Role of the parents		
Self-discipline and motivation		
Student interest in learning		

2 *Discuss the following questions in a small group. After your discussion, share your ideas with the class.*

1. Sir Christopher Ball predicted that the education system of the future would include a global curriculum and a worldwide qualifications system. What do you think he means? Do you think a global curriculum would improve or hurt the education system? Do you think a worldwide qualifications system is fair? Why or why not?

2. Margaret Rudland, head teacher of Godolphin and Latymer School, Hammersmith, said children needed to experience the "rough and tumble" of peer associations. What does she mean and how does this apply to home schooling? Do you agree that children need this experience?

B   READING TWO: *The Fun They Had*

The following story was written by Isaac Asimov in 1951. It addresses the question of home schooling using a computer. At that time, this type of home schooling was regarded as science fiction.

Read the first three paragraphs. Write short answers to the following questions. Then read the rest of the story.

1. What do you think was one of Isaac Asimov's fears about the future of books?

_____

_____

_____

2. Do you think we are headed in the direction he feared?

_____

_____

_____

THE FUN THEY HAD

BY ISAAC ASIMOV
(from *Earth Is Room Enough*)

1   Margie even wrote about it that night in her diary. On the page headed May 17, 2157, she wrote, "Today Tommy found a real book!"

2   It was a very old book. Margie's grandfather once said that when he was a little boy, his grandfather told him that there was a time when all stories were printed on paper.

3   They turned the pages, which were yellow and crinkly,[1] and it was awfully funny to read words that stood still instead of moving the way that they were supposed to—on a screen, you know. And then, when they had turned back to the page before, it had the same words on it that it had had when they read it the first time.

4   "Gee," said Tommy, "what a waste. When you're through with the book, you just throw it away, I guess. Our television screen must have had a million books on it and it's good for plenty more. I wouldn't throw it away."

5   "Same with mine," said Margie. She was eleven and hadn't seen as many books as Tommy had. He was thirteen.

6   She said, "Where did you find it?"

7   "In my house." He pointed without looking, because he was busy reading. "In the attic."

8   "What's it about?"

9   "School."

10   Margie was scornful. "School? What's there to write about school? I hate school."

11   Margie had always hated school, but now she hated it more than ever. The mechanical teacher[2] had been giving her test after test in geography

---

[1] *crinkly:* dried out
[2] *mechanical teacher:* a computer [in this story]

and she had been doing worse and worse until her mother had shaken her head sorrowfully and sent for the County Inspector.

12   He was a round little man with a red face and a whole box of tools with dials and wires. He smiled at Margie and gave her an apple, then took the teacher apart. Margie hoped he wouldn't know how to put it together again, but he knew how all right, and after an hour or so, there it was again, large and square and ugly, with a big screen on which all the lessons were shown and the questions were asked. That wasn't so bad. The part Margie hated most was the slot[3] where she had to put homework and test papers. She always had to write them out in a punch code they made her learn when she was six years old, and the mechanical teacher calculated the mark[4] in no time.

13   The Inspector had smiled after he was finished and patted Margie's head. He said to her mother, "It's not the little girl's fault, Mrs. Jones. I think the geography sector[5] was geared a little too quick. Those things happen sometimes. I've slowed it up to a ten-year level. Actually, the overall pattern of her progress is quite satisfactory." And he patted Margie's head again.

14   Margie was disappointed. She had been hoping they would take the teacher away altogether. They had once taken Tommy's teacher away for nearly a month because the history sector had blanked out[6] completely.

15   So she said to Tommy, "Why would anyone write about school?"

16   Tommy looked at her with very superior eyes. "Because it's not our kind of school, stupid. This is the old kind of school that they had hundreds and hundreds of years ago." He added loftily, pronouncing the word very carefully, "Centuries ago."

17   Margie was hurt. "Well, I don't know what kind of school they had all that time ago." She read the book over his shoulder for a while, then said, "Anyway, they had a teacher."

18   "Sure they had a teacher, but it wasn't a regular teacher. It was a man."

19   "A man? How could a man be a teacher?"

20   "Well, he just told the boys and girls things and gave them homework and asked them questions."

21   "A man isn't smart enough."

22   "Sure he is. My father knows as much as my teacher."

23   "He can't. A man can't know as much as a teacher."

24   "He knows almost as much, I betcha."[7]

25   Margie wasn't prepared to dispute that. She said, "I wouldn't want a strange man in my house to teach me."

---

[3] *slot:* an opening
[4] *mark:* a number or letter that shows how well a person does in school; a grade
[5] *sector:* area
[6] *blanked out:* been erased
[7] *I betcha:* "I'll bet you", "I'm sure"

26   Tommy screamed with laughter. "You don't know much, Margie. The teachers didn't live in the house. They had a special building and all the kids went there."

27   "And all the kids learned the same thing?"

28   "Sure, if they were the same age."

29   "But my mother says a teacher has to be adjusted to fit the mind of each boy and girl it teaches and that each kid has to be taught differently."

30   "Just the same, they didn't do it that way then. If you don't like it, you don't have to read the book."

31   "I didn't say I didn't like it," Margie said quickly. She wanted to read about those funny schools.

32   They weren't even half-finished when Margie's mother called, "Margie! School!"

33   Margie looked up. "Not yet, Mama."

34   "Now!" said Mrs. Jones. "And it's probably time for Tommy, too."

35   Margie said to Tommy, "Can I read the book some more with you after school?"

36   "Maybe," he said nonchalantly.[8] He walked away whistling, the dusty old book tucked beneath his arm.

37   Margie went into the schoolroom. It was right next to her bedroom and the mechanical teacher was on and waiting for her. It was always on at the same time every day except Saturday and Sunday, because her mother said little girls learned better if they learned at regular hours.

38   The screen was lit up, and it said: "Today's arithmetic lesson is on the addition of proper fractions. Please insert yesterday's homework in the proper slot."

39   Margie did so with a sigh. She was thinking about the old schools they had when her grandfather's grandfather was a little boy. All the kids from the whole neighborhood came, laughing and shouting in the schoolyard, sitting together in the schoolroom, going home together at the end of the day. They learned the same things, so they could help one another on the homework and talk about it.

40   And the teachers were people . . .

41   The mechanical teacher was flashing on the screen: "When we add the fractions 1/2 and 1/4—"

42   Margie was thinking about how the kids must have loved it in the old days. She was thinking of the fun they had.

---

[8] *nonchalantly:* casually, in an informal way

Discuss the following questions in small groups. Then share your ideas with the class.

1. Margie says that kids had fun in "the old days." What do you think Margie thought was fun? Do you agree? Why or why not?

2. Do you believe that schools today are headed in the direction of the home schooling described in "The Fun They Had"? If yes, how? If no, why not?

C LINKING READINGS ONE AND TWO

1 *Both Reading One and Reading Two describe home schooling. In what ways are they similar to and different from each other? With a partner, complete the chart comparing the readings.*

	READING ONE	READING TWO
1. Is there a teacher? If yes, describe the teacher.		
2. Where does the "school" take place?		
3. Who determines what the students learn and at what pace they learn?		
4. Who monitors the progress of the students?		
5. When and where do students socialize with friends?		
6. How do the students feel about home school compared to traditional school?		

2 *Work in a small group. Discuss the following questions. Then choose one of the questions and write your own response.*

1. What do you think are the biggest advantages of home schooling? What do you think are the biggest problems facing home-schooled students? What solutions can you think of for the problems?

2. How would home schooling or traditional schooling meet the three requirements for educational success mentioned in Sharing Information on page 140?

3. Would you rather be home-schooled by a family member or by a computer via the Internet? Why?

3 Focus on Vocabulary

1 *Read this information about British and American spelling.*

Reading One is from a British newspaper. Many words are spelled differently than in American English. In the late 1700s, Noah Webster, an American schoolteacher, published a book called *The American Spelling Book*. In this book, he attempted to simplify British spelling by dropping the *u* in words like *colour* and *harbour*. In addition, he changed *centre* to *center*, and *traveller* to *traveler*. Unfortunately, Webster was not consistent. Words like *glamour* and *acre* never changed from their British spelling. In addition, in the United States, many words have both an accepted British and American spelling, such as *grey/gray* and *axe/ax*.

Complete the chart with the British or American equivalent of the words listed. If you need help, use a dictionary. Discuss the spellings with your classmates.

BRITISH SPELLING	AMERICAN SPELLING
specialise	*specialize*
institutionalised	
behaviour	
	honor
	canceled
connexion	
learnt	
neighbour	
mediaeval	
	spelled
memorise	
	equaling
smelt	
	theater
defence	

Do you see any patterns? What rules can you figure out for changing British to American spelling?

_____

_____

_____

_____

_____

2 *Complete the chart with the different forms of the words found in the readings. Not all of the words have all four forms. If you need help, use a dictionary. After you have completed the chart, complete the crossword puzzle on the following page using the correct form of the words from the chart.*

NOUN	VERB	ADJECTIVE	ADVERB
freedom	*free*	*free*	*freely*
		bullying	X
	constrict		X
	X	curious	
		disappointed	
		disillusioned	X
		doubtful	
isolation			X
	X	lonely	X
relationship			X
rigidity	X		
	X	self-confident	
X	stifle		X
		surprised	
withdrawal			X

Across

1. Parents don't want their children to feel _____ by the rigid curricula of traditional schools.

2. Margie _____ that a man could be a teacher.

3. Hundreds of children are leaving traditional schools because of their parents' _____ with their children's education.

Down

4. Ms. Barson thinks the whole idea of educating children is to help them to be more _____.

5. Despite what critics of home schooling say, not all home-schooled students are shy and _____.

6. Many parents worry that home-schooled children will feel _____ from their peers.

7. The fact that a traditional school curriculum is so _____ has led many parents to decide to home-school their children.

8. Studying by herself made Margie feel _____.

3 *How do you think these people would answer the questions? Read the question and write their answer, using the words given. Change the word form or tense if necessary. Share your answers with a partner.*

1. To Professor Meighan:
   What do you think will happen to schools in the next twenty years?

   obsolete   outdate   constrict   stifle

   I believe that present-day schools will become obsolete and outdated.

   Schools these days constrict the students' freedom and stifle their

   creativity.

2. To Luis Barson, home schooler:
   What do you like about home schooling?

   freedom   peer pressure   bullying   self-confidence

   _____

   _____

   _____

3. To Leslie Barson, home schoolers' mother:
   Why are you so unhappy with traditional schools?

   disillusioned   disappointed   teaching methods   rigidity

   _____

   _____

   _____

4. To Professor Michael Barber:
   What concerns do you have about home schooling?

   isolation   withdrawal   peers   relationships

   _____

   _____

   _____

5. To Margie, from "The Fun They Had":
   What do you think about twentieth-century schools?

   doubtful   surprised   curious   lonely

   _____

   _____

   _____

4 Focus on Writing

A   GRAMMAR: Direct and Indirect Speech

1 *Examine the following sets of sentences and answer the questions with a partner.*

Direct Speech	Indirect Speech
• Professor Roland Meighan said, "Schools have become an outdated concept."	• Professor Roland Meighan said that schools had become an outdated concept.
• Professor Meighan said, "Schools will become obsolete."	• Professor Meighan said that schools would become obsolete.
• He said, "I believe children need experience."	• He said that he believed children needed experience.

1. What are the differences in punctuation between direct and indirect speech?

2. What other differences are there between direct and indirect speech? Which words are different? Can you explain how they change?

Direct and Indirect Speech

Speech (and writing) can be reported in two ways:

Direct speech (also called quoted speech) reports the speaker's exact words.
Indirect speech (also called reported speech) reports what the speaker said without using the exact words.

Punctuation

For direct speech, put quotation marks before and after the words being quoted. Use a comma to separate the words in quotation marks from the reporting verbs such as *say, tell,* and *report*.

For indirect speech, there is no special punctuation.

Verb Tense Changes

For indirect speech, when the reporting verb is in the past tense (***said, told, reported***), the verbs inside the quotation marks change. Here are some examples:

Direct Speech	Indirect Speech
Margie said, "I **do** my homework at night."	Margie said she **did** her homework at night

do/does (simple present)	→	**did** (simple past)
am/is/are doing (present progressive)	→	**was/were doing** (past progressive)
did (simple past)	→	**had done** (past perfect)
was/were doing (past progressive)	→	**had been doing** (past perfect progressive)
has/have done (present perfect)	→	**had done** (past perfect)
will (modal)	→	**would** (past modal)
can (modal)	→	**could** (past modal)
may (modal)	→	**might** (past modal)

Time and Location Changes

For indirect speech, time and location phrases may change to keep the speaker's original meaning.

Direct Speech	**Indirect Speech**
Tommy said," I don't have to study **now**."	Tommy said he didn't have to study **at that time.**

now	→	**then/at that time**
tomorrow	→	**the next (following) day**
ago	→	**before/earlier**
here	→	**there**
this	→	**that**

Pronouns and Possessives

For indirect speech, pronouns and possessives change to keep the speaker's original meaning.

Direct Speech	**Indirect Speech**
Mrs. Barson said," **I** …"	Mrs. Barson said **she** …
Mrs. Barson said,"**Our** children …"	Mrs. Barson said **their** children …

2 *Read the first sentence in each item. It is reported speech. Circle the letter of the speaker's exact words.*

1. She said that she learned more outside of school than she did in school.
   a. "I have learned more outside of school than I have in school."
   b. "I had learned more outside of school than I did in school."
   c. "I learn more outside of school than I do in school."

2. She reported that Luis had never attended school.
   a. "Luis has never attended school."
   b. "Luis never attends school."
   c. "Luis may never attend school."

3. He said that in order to succeed in life, he had to do well in school.
   a. "In order to succeed in life, I will have to do well in school."
   b. "In order to succeed in life, I have to do well in school."
   c. "In order to succeed in life, I have had to do well in school."

4. Professor Michael Barber told us that pupils would spend half their time at school and half at home.
   a. "Pupils spend half their time at school and half at home."
   b. "Pupils spent half their time at school and half at home."
   c. "Pupils will spend half their time at school and half at home."

5. Margaret Rudland said that students at her school felt that they might benefit from some home schooling.
   a. "Students at my school feel that they benefited from some home schooling."
   b. "Students at my school feel that they may benefit from some home schooling."
   c. "Students at my school feel that they will benefit from some home schooling."

6. Professor Meighan reported that many students were studying at home.
   a. "Many students are studying at home."
   b. "Many students studied at home."
   c. "Many students had been studying at home."

7. Margie said that they hadn't had time to think about the book.
   a. "We don't have time to think about the book."
   b. "We didn't have time to think about the book."
   c. "We may not have time to think about the book."

3 *Change the following direct speech to indirect speech. Remember to keep the speaker's original meaning.*

1. Tommy said, "My father knows as much as my teacher."

   Tommy said his father knew as much as his teacher.

   _____

2. The inspector told Margie's mother, "I think the geography sector was a little too difficult."

   _____

   _____

3. He added, "I've slowed it up to a ten-year level."

   _____

   _____

4. Tommy said, "This is the old kind of school that they had hundreds and hundreds of years ago."

   _____

   _____

5. Margie told Tommy, "My mother says a teacher has to be adjusted to fit the mind of each boy and girl it teaches."

   _____

   _____

6. Tommy told Margie, "You can read the book with me again tomorrow."

   _____

   _____

B STYLE: Concessions

1 *Read the following letter and discuss the questions with a partner.*

Dear Editor:

"Inadequately prepared parents" and "weak curricula" are two of the main concerns critics have of home schooling. As a home-schooled student, I would like to address these concerns. During my third and fourth grade years, I was taken out of school to be taught by my mother. When I was put back in school at the beginning of fifth grade, I was at the head of my class. Although my mother was not a trained teacher, she was not only able to keep up with the material, but also enjoyed learning and exploring the material with me. Moreover, despite the fact that traditional school teachers are highly qualified, it seems they waste a lot of time disciplining students rather than actually teaching them.

Critics say that home schoolers have a weak curriculum. This issue is true of public schools as well. I was actually taken out of public school because the curricula did not challenge me. In addition, I would like to point out that even though home schoolers are not under the rigid curricula of traditional schools, they often spend more time on the subjects or topics that really interest them. Because of this, children can actually learn more than what the curriculum requires. Furthermore, for many home schoolers, learning is not confined just to the home. In fact, learning takes place everywhere and all the time: at museums, during family vacations—twelve months a year! This may explain why home-taught students are doing 25 percent better than the state's public school average.

In conclusion, I believe our educational system must rise to the highest level that it can so that we students remain in school and remain interested in learning. When that finally happens, maybe we won't need to be home schooled. By the way, I'm at home again.

—Max Andrew Jacobs, Grade 11
Amarillo, Texas

1. Which of the two types of schooling described in the letter does the writer prefer?

2. What two concerns about home schooling does the writer address?

3. How does the writer defend these concerns—by presenting only his opinion, or by acknowledging the side of the traditional schools and then presenting his own opinion?

4. Which opinion do the words *although, even though,* and *despite the fact* introduce? Do they introduce the opinion of the traditional school or the home school?

Concessions

When expressing your opinion, it is important to support your opinion but, at the same time, recognize and describe the opposing opinion. Admitting similarities and differences in contrasting points of view can make your argument stronger.

Concession Clauses

- The following words are used to concede or acknowledge similarities or differences between two contrasting ideas.

  although   in spite of the fact that

  though   despite the fact that

  even though

- Note that these words do not introduce a complete thought—they introduce dependent clauses. They need a main independent clause to complete the sentence. The main clause usually describes the point that is more important.

  Although my mother was not a trained teacher, she was able to keep up with the material.

  Writer's opinion: My mother was not a trained teacher, but she had no problems keeping up with the material.

  Opposing position: Only trained teachers should teach children.

  Even though home schoolers are not under the rigid curricula of traditional schools, they often spend more time on the subjects or topics that really interest them.

  Writer's opinion: Home schoolers learn more because they can spend more time on the topics that interest them.

  Opposing position: Children learn more under the controlled curricula of traditional schools.

Punctuation

- When the sentence begins with the dependent clause, a comma separates it from the main clause.

  Although my mother was not a trained teacher, she was able to keep up with the material.

- When the sentence begins with the independent clause, there is no comma.

  My mother was able to keep up with the material **although she was not a trained teacher.**

2 *Combine each pair of sentences using the words in parentheses. After you have written your sentence, indicate whether it supports home schooling or traditional schooling.*

1. Supporters of home schooling say that the children have enough social contact. Critics say children should be in a school setting surrounded by peers.

   (even though)

   Supporters of home schooling say that the children have enough social

   contact even though they are not in a school setting surrounded by peers.

   (supports home schooling)/ supports traditional schooling

2. Critics maintain that there is no way to assess home schoolers. Supporters of home schooling say that they are following a standard curriculum.

   (though)

   _____

   _____

   _____

   supports home schooling/ supports traditional schooling

3. Critics question whether home schoolers are being taught the basics. Home schoolers are gaining in numbers every year.

   (although)

   _____

   _____

   _____

   supports home schooling/ supports traditional schooling

4. Critics worry that traditional school students do not take school seriously. Many successful students graduate from traditional schools every year.

   (in spite of the fact that)

   _____

   _____

   _____

   supports home schooling/ supports traditional schooling

5. Home schooling is apparently very successful. Many people still believe in the benefits of traditional schooling.

(despite the fact that)

_____

_____

_____

supports home schooling/ supports traditional schooling

3 *For each educational issue below, write a sentence that expresses your opinion while showing concession to the other position. Use the concession words or phrases in the box and the words in each item. After you have written your sentence, indicate whether it supports home schooling or traditional schooling.*

although though	even though despite the fact that	in spite of the fact that

1. **peer pressure**

   Although students in traditional schools experience more peer pressure

   and bullying, they also learn how to socialize with their peers.

   _____

   supports home schooling/(supports traditional schooling)

2. **teaching methods**

   _____

   _____

   _____

   supports home schooling/ supports traditional schooling

3. **curriculum**

   _____

   _____

   _____

   supports home schooling/ supports traditional schooling

4. teacher qualifications

_____

_____

_____

supports home schooling/ supports traditional schooling

5. students' self-discipline and self-motivation

_____

_____

_____

supports home schooling/ supports traditional schooling

6. students' interest in learning

_____

_____

_____

supports home schooling/ supports traditional schooling

C WRITING TOPICS

Write an essay expressing your opinion about one of these topics. Be sure to use some of the ideas, vocabulary, grammar, and style that you have learned in this unit.

1. Do you think home schooling is a good idea? Why or why not?

2. Do you believe that teachers are the most important factor in a student's success? Why or why not?

3. Do you believe that peer pressure weakens a student's ability to learn? Why or why not?

4. Look back at the three requirements identified by the quiz in Sharing Information on page 140. Which do you believe is the most important to a student's success? Why? Are there other requirements you feel are more important?

D RESEARCH TOPIC

Report on home schooling.

Step 1: Work in a small group. Choose a home schooling organization you would like to research. Go to the library or use the Internet (key words *home school* or *home schooling*). See reference list below for ideas.

Step 2: Prepare a list of questions you would like to answer as you research home schooling.

Step 3: Share your research with your group. Combine your information and write a group report using this basic outline. Present your report to the class.

> Part I: Introduction
> - A brief introduction to your topic (home schooling)
> - An explanation of what information you were looking for (your original questions)
> - An explanation of where and how you found your information
>
> Part II: Results
> - The information you collected and the answers to your questions
>
> Part III: Conclusions
> - Final conclusions and opinions you have about home schooling

Reference List

American Homeschool Association
P.O. Box 3142
Palmer, AK 99645
tel. 800-236-3278
www.americanhomeschoolassociation.com

Homeschool World
www.home-school.com

Home Education Network, also called Alternative Education Resource Group
c/7 Bartlett St.
Moorabbin, VIC 3189
Australia
tel. (03) 553-4720
www.home-ed.vic.edu.au

Ontario Federation of Teaching Parents
83 Fife Rd.
Guelph, Ontario, N1H 6X9
Canada
www.ontariohomeschool.org

Education Otherwise
36 Kinross Rd.
Leamington Spa, Warwickshire, CV32 7EF
England
tel. (0926) 886828
www.education-otherwise.org

Rhein Main Homeschoolers
c/o AAFES
PSC 05, Box 2134
APO AE 09057
Germany
tel. 49-6150-14788
06150-14788 (in Germany)

Otherwise Japan
P.O. Kugayama Suginami-ku
Tokyo, Japan
tel. 81 3-3331-6554
jab02521@nifyserve.or.jp

For step-by-step practice in the writing process, see the *Writing Activity Book, High Intermediate,* Unit 7.

Assignment	Classification essay
Prewriting	Classifying
Organizing	Explaining classifications
Revising	Using concession clauses to acknowledge opposing points of view
	Using direct and indirect speech
Editing	Using word forms for coherence

For Unit 7 Internet activities, visit the NorthStar Companion Website at
http://www.longman.com/northstar

Eat to Live or Live to Eat?

1 Focus on the Topic

A PREDICTING

Look at the photographs and the title of the unit. Then discuss these questions with a partner.

1. What do the photographs show? What are the people doing? How do you think they feel?

2. What are the similarities and differences between the two photos?

3. What do you think the title of the unit means? What do you think this unit will be about?

B SHARING INFORMATION

1 *What is the most memorable meal you have ever had? Interview three classmates. Ask about their most memorable meal. Complete the chart with your notes.*

	YOU	CLASSMATE 1	CLASSMATE 2	CLASSMATE 3
What was the meal?				
Where was it eaten?				
Who was at the meal?				
Why was it so memorable?				

2 *Share your information with the class. Make a list of common reasons why meals are memorable. Is it the food? The place? The people?*

C PREPARING TO READ

BACKGROUND

Chuck Williams, founder of Williams-Sonoma, a U.S. chain of cookware stores, says this about cooking in the next decade.

"It's [cooking is] headed toward easier and more convenient cooking. I don't think people will let their favorite dishes disappear, but the kind of cooking done by our grandmothers will. People just don't have the time and there are too many alternatives. People used to cook three meals a day because they had to, even if they did not like to cook. Now there are other options. People today cook on the weekends to entertain."

Answer these questions with a partner.

1. What kind of cooking does he mean by "the kind of cooking done by our grandmothers"? Do you agree or disagree? Why or why not?

2. Read the following U.S. statistics on food and cooking. Choose whether the information is true or not for you and explain why.

Cooking on the weekend
Weekend cooking is becoming more and more popular. Of the people surveyed, 41 percent cook a big meal on Sunday and 15 percent cook a big meal on Saturday. *(National Pork Producers Council)*

For you: true/ not true _____

Spending time in the kitchen
According to 48 percent of the people surveyed, spending an hour or more to prepare a meal on the weekends was fine with them. Only 37 percent were willing to spend the same amount of time on a weeknight. People said they enjoyed cooking on the weekends as a way to spend quality time with family and friends. *(National Pork Producers Council)*

For you: true/ not true _____

Food dollars spent away from home
Approximately 38–40 percent of food dollars are spent away from home. *(National Restaurant Association)*

For you: true/ not true _____

VOCABULARY FOR COMPREHENSION

Guess the meaning of the underlined words from the context of the following sentences. Circle the letter of the word or phrase that is closest in meaning.

1. Our food is <u>inextricably linked with</u> manners, with form, with tradition, with history. It is a part of every aspect of our lives.
   a. strongly tied to
   b. separated from
   c. somewhat connected to

2. He would show me the correct way to prepare rice, telling me that if our rice was old then perhaps more water than <u>customary</u> might be needed to give our congee[1] its fine and silky finish. He meant you had to add more than the typical amount of water.
   a. extraordinary
   b. natural
   c. normal

3. The <u>ramifications</u> of cooking were very important to my grandmother. In other words, everything connected with cooking—the ingredients, the process, and the results—had special meaning to her.
   a. effects
   b. origins
   c. recipes

---

[1] *congee:* a thick rice porridge

4. They and my Ah Paw, my mother's mother, <u>insisted</u> that I be involved in our family table. It was not a choice.

   a. believed
   b. demanded
   c. warned

5. My grandmother knew instinctively, without ever having had to personally put a spatula into a wok,[2] how things ought to be cooked, what foods <u>wedded</u> in combination, and what clashed. Her ability to combine tastes made her an exceptional cook.

   a. melted
   b. conflicted
   c. went well together

6. I liked her home, I liked her kitchen, and she <u>spoiled</u> me. She provided me with everything I ever wanted or needed.

   a. cleaned
   b. understood
   c. treated very well or too well

7. She would eat no vegetables that were older than two hours out of the ground, which <u>necessitated</u> repeated trips to the markets. The servants had to go shopping more than once a day.

   a. required
   b. avoided
   c. attracted

8. She <u>cautioned</u> me to eat every kernel[3] of rice in my bowl, for if I did not, she warned, the man I married would have a pockmarked[4] face. Warnings like these were hard to ignore.

   a. told
   b. strongly advised
   c. ordered

9. My grandmother was an observant Buddhist who declined to eat either fish or meat on the first and the fifteenth of each month and for the first fifteen days of the New Year, and our family ate similarly out of <u>deference</u> to her. We tried to support her religious beliefs as much as we could.

   a. fear
   b. respect
   c. love

---

[2] *wok:* a Chinese cooking pan
[3] *kernel (of rice):* piece of rice
[4] *pockmarked:* covered with scars made by a skin disease

2 Focus on Reading

A   READING ONE: *The Chinese Kitchen*

Eileen Yin-Fei Lo is a cooking teacher and cookbook writer. In the reading, she celebrates the cooking traditions of her native China as she remembers her childhood days growing up in her family's kitchen.

Read the first paragraph. Write three questions that you think will be answered in the reading. Then read the rest of the story.

1. _____

2. _____

3. _____

THE CHINESE KITCHEN

BY EILEEN YIN-FEI LO
(from The Chinese Kitchen)

1   Food is not only life-giving but also a source of familial or societal leanings.[1] Our food is inextricably linked with manners, with form, with tradition, with history. I grew up with these beliefs. I remember my father, Lo Pak Wan, my first cooking teacher, telling me that we must eat our food first with our eyes, then with our minds, then with our noses, and finally with our mouths. He believed this. He taught this to my brother and me.

2   He would say, only partly joking, that fine vegetables should be chosen with as much care as one would a

_____

[1] *leanings:* tendency to agree with certain beliefs

son-in-law. He would show me the correct way to prepare rice, telling me that if our rice was old then perhaps more water than customary might be needed to give our congee[2] its fine and silky finish. "Keep an open mind," he would say. "Cook the way it has been written, but keep an open mind. If you keep walking only in a straight line, you will go into a wall. You must learn to make a turn if necessary. Do not be narrow." Or he would tell me, "*Tau mei haw yan tiu, mo mei haw yan tiu,*" an aphorism[3] that translates as "if you don't have a tail, you cannot imitate the monkey; if you do have a tail, then do not imitate the monkey." By this he was telling me to follow the classical manner but not to be a simple, mindless imitator.

3   My mother, Lo Chan Miu Hau, encouraged me to cook as well. I recall her saying to me, "If you are wealthy and know how to cook, then servants cannot take advantage of you. If you are poor and know how to cook, you will be able to create wonderful meals with few resources." Cooking and its ramifications were that important to her, as well as to my father, when I was young and growing up in Sun Tak, a suburb of Canton, now Guangzhou.

4   They and my Ah Paw, my mother's mother, insisted that I be involved in our family table. Ah Paw, despite her household of servants, despite the presence of a family cook, made certain whenever I visited her, which was every opportunity I had, every school holiday, that I was in her kitchen.

5   My Ah Paw knew instinctively, without ever having had to personally put a spatula into a wok,[4] how things ought to be cooked, what foods wedded in combination, and what clashed. I am tempted to suggest that she was a brilliant, instinctive kitchen chemist. I will say it. Brilliant she was indeed, her knowledge about foods was encyclopedic, and she was never wrong about cooking, then or now, in my memory. I spent much of the Lunar New Year at her house. I liked her home, I liked her kitchen, and she spoiled me. Except when it came to imparting cookery lessons.

6   When we ate raw fish, *yue sahng*, she taught, one had to prepare the fish in the proper manner. You hit the fish at the front of its head to stun it, then, when it was still nominally alive, you scaled it, gutted and cleaned it, then sliced it for eating. This special dish, which we ate on important birthdays, and on the eves of family weddings, had to be prepared this way, only this way, Ah Paw said.

7   When we steamed a fish, she taught me to softly lay the fish atop a bed of rice at the precise moment that the rice was in the final state of its absorption of water. It would then be perfectly prepared.

8   Once I steamed a fish, quite well, I thought, and proudly carried it to her at the family table. She sniffed. I had forgotten to pour boiled

[2] *congee:* a thick rice porridge
[3] *aphorism:* saying, expression
[4] *wok:* a Chinese cooking pan

peanut oil over it just before serving. "Take it back to the kitchen and add the oil", she ordered. My grandmother's kitchen always had a crock of boiled peanut oil near the stove. To pour it over fish was to give the fish fragrance and to dispel[5] any unpleasant odors. It does, even if the oil is not warm.

9   She would eat no vegetables that were older than two hours out of the ground, which necessitated repeated trips to the markets by her servants, a lesson of the importance of freshness that was not lost on me.

10   She cautioned me to eat every kernel[6] of rice in my bowl, for if I did not, she warned, the man I married would have a pockmarked[7] face, one mark for each uneaten rice kernel. I did as she cautioned, and I must have eaten well, for my husband's face is clear.

11   Do not shout in the kitchen, Ah Paw would insist. Do not use improper words in the kitchen. Do not show shortness of temper in the kitchen by, for example, banging chopsticks[8] on a wok. All of these would reflect badly on us as a family, she would say, when done in front of Jo Kwan, the Kitchen God, whose image hung on the wall over the oven. For just before the Lunar New Year the image of Jo Kwan, his lips smeared with honey, was always burned so that he would go up to heaven and report only nice things about our family.

12   Ah Paw would consult her Tung Sing, an astrological book, for propitious[9] days on which to begin preparing the special dumplings we made and ate during the New Year festival. She would specify to the second time to make the dough, heat the oven, add the oil, in what we called "*hoi yau wok*," or, literally translated, "begin the oil in the wok." So admired was she for her knowledge that young married couples, not even of our family, would consult with her. A memory I have is of pumping the pedal of the iron and stone grinding mill in our town square, at her orders, to get the flour that we would use for our dumplings.

13   She was an observant Buddhist who declined to eat either fish or meat on the first and the fifteenth of each month and for the first fifteen days of the New Year, and our family ate similarly out of deference to her. She was happy that my mother always encouraged me to cook, happy that my father brought kitchen discipline to me as well. She nodded with pleasure, in support of my father, I remember—not in sympathy with me—when I complained how boring it was when my father gave me the task of snapping off the ends of individual mung bean sprouts. "If you wish to learn how to make spring rolls[10] well, learn the beginning of the spring roll. It must be done," Ah Paw said.

---

[5] *dispel:* to stop someone believing or feeling something; chase away
[6] *kernel (of rice):* piece of rice
[7] *pockmarked:* covered with scars made by a skin disease
[8] *chopsticks:* a pair of thin sticks used for eating food, especially by people in Asia
[9] *propitious:* favorable, likely to bring good results
[10] *spring roll:* cooked vegetables wrapped in a special dough

14   We had no grinders.[11] We chopped meats and other seafood with the cleaver[12] on a chopping board. "Clean it," Ah Paw would say when I was finished. "If you do not, the food you chop next will not stick together. It will fall apart. There will be no texture. If it falls apart, I will know that you did not listen."

15   All of this she conferred on me without ever setting foot in the kitchen of her house. As a further example of her vision I should note in passing that my Ah Paw, a most independent woman, as is evident, refused to have bound the feet of my mother, her daughter, much the practice of high born women. This despite the fact that her own feet had been bound since babyhood and were no more than four inches long. This extraordinary woman, never more than seventy-five pounds, who could not totter more than one hundred feet and was usually carried by servants, brought my mother and then me into modern times in her own way. I wanted nothing more than to be with her, and I would listen, wide-eyed and receptive, to her talk about food and its meanings . . . .

[11] *grinder:* machine which chops up food
[12] *cleaver:* heavy chopping knife

READING FOR MAIN IDEAS

1 *Eileen Yin-Fei Lo talks about the three people who influenced her cooking most. Complete the sentences with information describing why each person was important to her.*

• Her father was important because _____

_____

_____

• Her mother was important because _____

_____

_____

• Her grandmother was important because _____

_____

_____

2 *Answer the following question about Yin-Fei Lo's family: What influenced their cooking practices and techniques?*

_____

_____

_____

READING FOR DETAILS

The author talks about how, in her family, food is linked with cooking processes, traditions, superstitions, and religious beliefs. Complete the chart with an example of each from the reading. Write the number of the paragraph where you found your example.

COOKING PROCESS	TRADITION	SUPERSTITION	RELIGIOUS BELIEF
Paragraph _____	Paragraph _____	Paragraph _____	Paragraph _____

REACTING TO THE READING

1 *Write true (T) or false (F) for each sentence. Write the number of the paragraph that supports your answer. If the statement is false, correct it on the line provided.*

_____ 1. The author's mother thought being able to cook was important for all people, rich and poor.

Paragraph Number _____

Correction: _____

_____ 2. Ah Paw was an experienced cook.

Paragraph Number _____

Correction: _____

_____ 3. The author's father believed you should never change a recipe.

Paragraph Number _____

Correction: _____

_____ 4. In Ah Paw's house, any food could be prepared and eaten at any time of the year.

Paragraph Number _____

Correction: _____

_____ 5. It was well known that Ah Paw was very knowledgeable about cooking.

Paragraph Number _____

Correction: _____

_____ 6. Ah Paw was very demanding concerning the quality of food she ate.

Paragraph Number _____

Correction: _____

_____ 7. At Ah Paw's house, the servants helped with the preparation of the food.

Paragraph Number _____

Correction: _____

_____ 8. The author's father believed in the importance of choosing vegetables carefully.

Paragraph Number _____

Correction: _____

2 *Look back at Reading for Details on page 175. Think about cooking practices in your own culture and write an example from your culture for each of the following. Note the similarities and the differences between Yin-Fei Lo's culture and yours. Share your answers with the class.*

cooking process: _____

_____

_____

tradition: _____

_____

_____

superstition: _____

_____

_____

religious belief: _____

_____

_____

B **READING TWO:** *"Slow Food" Movement Aims at Restoring the Joy of Eating*

Now that the twenty-first century has begun, it is clear that the pace of life is ever increasing. Nevertheless, some people around the world are consciously slowing down their pace, at least in the kitchen and at the table. They are embracing the idea of the importance of food and companionship at the table. People are also taking more interest in how food is grown, how it is prepared, and even how and with whom it is eaten. There is also a renewed interest in cultural food traditions. All of these issues are addressed in a new international food movement known as the "Slow Food" movement.

Discuss these questions with a partner.

1. The term "fast food" means food that is prepared quickly in order to save time. McDonald's, Pizza Hut, and Kentucky Fried Chicken are examples of fast food. Why do you think the movement you are going to read about is called "Slow Food"?

2. How do you think the people who support "Slow Food" feel about fast food?

"Slow Food" Movement Aims at Restoring the Joy of Eating

By Cathy Heiner (from *USA Today*)

1 "The Slow Food movement is committed to the preservation and restoration of a traditional convivial joy, the joy of the table," says Jonathan White, a member of the Slow Food organization and owner of Egg Farm Dairy in Peekskill, N.Y. "And that's not just about food and wine; it's also about kinship and companionship, which you just don't get going to a drive-through[1] and eating in traffic."

2 Whopper[2] lovers, don't have a meltdown. Slow Food may use a snail as its logo, but it's not anti-fast food. "We're not against anything," White says. "Our agenda is to educate people who don't

Slow Food®

know about the pleasures of the table and, through education, to help traditional food artisans—bakers, cheesemakers, farmers growing heirloom[3] vegetables—to survive by sustaining demand for their product."

3 Members of Slow Food meet for long, leisurely meals. They talk food, wine, culture and philosophy. They organize wine

---

[1] *drive-through:* a fast-food restaurant with a car service window
[2] *Whopper:* a type of hamburger from Burger King
[3] *heirloom:* old-style and usually valuable

tastings and cooking classes. But most of all, they work to eradicate the "nuke[4] it and eat it" American lifestyle.

4   "Slow Food is not only about literally eating slowly, but also about savoring and appreciating the pleasures of good food and drink. Slow Food is "a way of life," says its Web site (www.slowfood.com).

5   The movement got cooking in the late 1980s when a fast-food burger joint[5] was about to open on Rome's beloved Piazza Spagna. A young Italian organization called Arcigola, dedicated to rediscovering and advocating authentic Italian traditions, protested. From the fray,[6] Slow Food was born.

6   "It was just a game at first," says founder Carlo Petrini, "a chance to remind people that food is a perishable[7] art, as pleasurable in its way as a sculpture by Michelangelo."

7   Today, Slow Food is 20,000 strong in Italy, where the joy of the table is a matter of national pride. And there are Slow Food organizations in more than 15 countries, from Switzerland to Singapore.

8   Although the movement is new to these shores, adherents say they believe Americans will take to it like pigs to truffles.[8] "Every year Americans are going to more restaurants, asking and learning more about food," says Paul Bartolotta, Slow Foodist and owner of Chicago's Spiaggia restaurant.

9   He says the USA is ripe for Slow Food. "Ten years ago, there were hardly any (farmers) markets, we were fast-food-driven, and there was less interest in food and wine. It has dramatically changed. Now there are organic supermarkets. There's a cultural awareness of what we're eating and why."

10   Slow Food could even tame America's obsession with dieting, White says. "If you only feed the body, you get fat. It's important not to deny the spiritual aspects of eating, to milk[9] the most joy out of the bodily function of eating."

11   And time at the table is time well spent, says Bartolotta. "The Slow Food movement's message is, 'Let's eat well and enjoy it.' No matter how crazy and hectic our lives are, the pleasure of the table is a fundamental right."

How to Slow Down

12   Can harried soccer moms[10] and overworked dads become Slow Foodists? How fast-food fanatics can add joy to their tables:

13   • **Turn off the TV.** "Cooking with your kids is a great family activity," says Jonathan White, a Slow Foodist from Peekskill, N.Y. "The preparation of food is one of the oldest human cultural traditions, and it's always been a parent-to-child thing."

14   • **Throw away the microwave.** "It's a myth when people say they don't have time to cook," says David Auerbach, leader of a chapter in Raleigh, N.C. "There's lots of good cookbooks that tell you how to make a meal in 30 minutes or less."

15   • **Shop at farmers markets.** "Get to know the growers," says Barbara Bowman, co-director of the Sonoma, Calif., chapter. The freshness of your food is guaranteed.

16   • **Perpetuate your family's traditions.** "Food, jokes, proverbs, toasts. Slow Food is not just about feasting; it's also about preserving traditions," Bowman says.

---

[4] *nuke:* to cook or heat something in a microwave
[5] *joint:* a slang word for place—usually a restaurant or bar
[6] *fray:* a conflict
[7] *perishable:* unpreserved and therefore able to decay or spoil quickly
[8] *like pigs to truffles:* enthusiastically
[9] *milk:* to get all the advantages you can from a situation
[10] *soccer moms:* a term used for mothers who spend a lot of time driving their children to and from sports games and other activities

17 • **Patronize**[11] **restaurants that specialize in local, regional cuisine.** "When traveling, eat what and where the locals eat," Bowman says.

To join, write to **Slow Food**, *c/o Egg Farm Dairy, 2 John Walsh Blvd., Peekskill, N.Y. 10566.*

---

[11] *patronize:* to support, go to

Copyright 1998, Gannett Co., Inc. Reprinted with permission.

Answer the following questions. Then share your answers with a partner.

1. How did the Slow Food movement begin?

2. What are the beliefs of the Slow Food movement?

3. Why is the United States ready for the Slow Food movement?

C LINKING READINGS ONE AND TWO

When Eileen Yin-Fei Lo was growing up, there was no such thing as a Slow Food movement. Nevertheless, there are many similarities between her food experiences and the Slow Food movement's beliefs. Complete the chart with examples of how Yin-Fei Lo's experiences relate to the Slow Food movement.

SLOW FOOD BELIEFS	EILEEN YIN-FEI LO'S FOOD TRADITIONS
1. Cooking: "Cooking with your kids is a great family activity. The preparation of food is one of the oldest human cultural traditions, and it's always been a parent-to-child thing."	Her father was her first cooking teacher. Her mother and grandmother also taught her about cooking. She spent many hours in her grandmother's kitchen.
2. Eating: "If you only feed the body, you get fat. It's important not to deny the spiritual aspects of eating, to milk the most joy out of the bodily function of eating."	
3. Food shopping: "Get to know the [local] growers." The freshness of your food is guaranteed.	
4. Family traditions: Perpetuate your family's traditions. "Food, jokes, proverbs, toasts. Slow Food is not just about feasting; it's also about preserving traditions."	

3 Focus on Vocabulary

1 *Look at these sentences from Readings One and Two. What do you notice about the underlined words? How do the underlined words relate to the verbs in the sentences?*

- Our food is <u>inextricably</u> linked with manners, with form, with tradition, with history. (verb)

- My Ah Paw knew <u>instinctively</u>, . . . how things ought to be cooked. (verb)

- It [the Slow Food Movement] has <u>dramatically</u> changed. (verb)

The underlined words are adverbs. Adverbs describe or give deeper meaning to verbs. Adverbs are usually formed by adding -*ly* to an adjective.

Adverbs can go in in several different places in a sentence. They can go: at the beginning of their clause, at the end of their clause, before a verb that is one word, and after the first helping verb.

Rewrite the following sentences using the adverbs given.

1. I eat the same thing for breakfast almost every day. I have a bowl of cereal, toast, and coffee.

(usually) *I usually eat the same thing for breakfast every day.*

2. Ah Paw had never gone into the kitchen and had never cooked anything, but she knew how foods should be cooked.

(personally) _____

3. At the market, the young farmer displayed the corn he had grown himself. He felt very good about his corn.

(proudly) _____

4. After trying again and again, Andy was able to bake a good loaf of bread. It was delicious and worth the effort he had to put into it.

(finally) _____

5. If you are quiet and listen carefully, you can hear the food sizzling in the wok.

(softly) _____

6. When Laura said *she had bigger fish to fry*, she wasn't talking about fish. She meant she had more important things to do.

(literally) _____

7. It was interesting to hear how you cook shrimp, but I don't agree with everything you said. I like to use more lemon and less salt.

(partly) _____

2 *Work in a small group. Read the following sentences. Circle the letter of the best explanation for each underlined phrasal verb.*

1. I <u>grew up</u> with these beliefs.
   a. got taller
   b. was born
   c. was raised

2. If you are wealthy and know how to cook, then servants cannot <u>take advantage of</u> you.
   a. help
   b. pay
   c. exploit

3. I liked her home, I liked her kitchen, and she spoiled me. Except when it <u>came to</u> imparting cookery lessons.
   a. involved
   b. arrived
   c. awoke

4. The image of Jo Kwan, his lips smeared with honey, was always burned so that he would <u>go up</u> to heaven and report only nice things about our family.
   a. worship
   b. rise
   c. drop

5. All of this she conferred on me without ever <u>setting foot in</u> the kitchen of her house.
   a. leaving
   b. dressing
   c. entering

6. Slow Foodists tell people to <u>turn off</u> their TV.
   a. dislike
   b. exit
   c. stop use of

7. They also say to <u>throw away</u> your microwave.
   a. get rid of
   b. improve
   c. arrange

8. Although the Slow Food movement is new here, followers say they believe
   we will <u>take to</u> it enthusiastically.
   a. control
   b. like
   c. bring

3 *Read this information and do the exercise that follows.*

Imagine a large international restaurant chain is proposing to build a fast-food restaurant in a community that presently has no fast-food restaurants. Think about the ramifications for the community. How will it affect small restaurant owners, employment opportunities, and quality of life? Will it improve the community or make it worse?

Divide the class into two groups. Group A is in favor of building a fast-food restaurant and writes six reasons why the restaurant is a good idea. Group B is against it and writes six reasons why it is a bad idea. Leave space under each reason so that a student from the other side can write a response.

Then, work in pairs with one student from Group A and one from Group B in each pair. Exchange papers with your partner and respond to each other's reasons. Use at least six words from the two vocabulary exercises above.

4 Focus on Writing

A GRAMMAR: Phrasal Verbs

1 *Examine the following sentences and answer the questions with a partner.*

    a. Slow Foodists say you should throw away your microwave.

    b. They also say you should turn off your television.

    c. Cooks constantly come up with new ideas of how to cook fish.

1. What is the verb in each sentence?

2. What is the difference between *throw* and *throw away*?

3. What is the difference between *turn* and *turn off*?

4. What is the difference between *come* and *come up with*?

Phrasal Verbs

A **phrasal verb** consists of a verb and a particle (an adverb or preposition). The combination of words often has a meaning that is very different from the meanings of its separate parts. Phrasal verbs are used more often in informal English than in formal English.

Forming Phrasal Verbs

- Phrasal verbs (also called two-part or two-word verbs) combine a verb with a particle.

VERB	+	PARTICLE	=	MEANING
take	+	back	=	return
look	+	over	=	examine
give	+	up	=	quit

- Some phrasal verbs (also called three-part or three-word verbs) combine with a preposition.

PHRASAL VERB	+	PREPOSITION	=	MEANING
come up	+	with	=	imagine or invent
think back	+	on	=	remember

- Some phrasal verbs are **transitive.** They take a direct object. Many (two-word) transitive phrasal verbs are separable. This means the verb and the particle can be separated by the direct object.

  She **looked over** the recipe.
  　　verb　particle　　object

  She **looked** the recipe **over**.
  　　verb　　　object　　particle

- However, when the direct object is a pronoun it <u>must</u> go between the verb and the particle.

  She **picked** it **up**.
  　　verb　object　particle

  　　But not

  ~~She picked up it.~~
  　　verb　particle　object

- Some phrasal verbs are **intransitive.** They do not take a direct object.

  I liked that restaurant. I want to **go back** next week.
  　　　　　　　　　　　　　　　　verb particle

(continued)

Using Phrasal Verbs

- The words in a phrasal verb are usually common, but their meaning changes when the words are used together. Therefore, it is not usually possible to guess the meaning of the verb from its individual parts.

  call off   =   cancel

  drop out of   =   quit

- Some phrasal verbs have more than one meaning.

  She **took off** her apron.   =   She **removed** her apron.

  She **took off** for the market at 7:00 A.M.   =   She **departed** for the market.

  She **took** the day **off** from cooking.   =   She **didn't** cook that day.

- Some verbs can be combined with different particles or prepositions. Each combination creates a phrasal verb with a different meaning.

  She **turned down** the heat in the oven.   =   She **lowered** the heat in the oven.

  She **turned on** the stove.   =   She **started** the stove.

  She **turned over** the fish in the pan.   =   She **flipped** the fish in the pan.

  A fast-food restaurant **turned up** on the Piazza Spagna in the 1980s.   =   A fast-food restaurant **appeared** on the Piazza Spagna in the 1980s.

2 Work in a small group. Complete the sentences with the word or phrase that has the same meaning as the underlined phrasal verb.

1. become popular   invent   got older   entered

   a. Eileen Yin-Fei Lo learned more and more about cooking as she <u>grew up</u>.
      got older

   b. Many experienced cooks are able to <u>come up with</u> a dinner after seeing what they have in their refrigerators. _____

   c. Although Ah Paw never <u>set foot in</u> the kitchen, she knew instinctively which spices were needed for a certain dish. _____

   d. The idea of cooking with natural organic ingredients is starting to <u>catch on</u> all over the world. _____

2. like   remove from   clean   get rid of

   a. When the soup is done, <u>take</u> it <u>off</u> the stove. _____

   b. After you finish cooking, you should always <u>pick up</u>, so you will be ready to cook again. _____

   c. Don't <u>throw away</u> the oil when you are finished cooking. You can use it again later. _____

   d. Americans are starting to <u>take to</u> the idea of dinner being a time the family should be together. _____

3. remember   exploit   eliminate   examine

   a. Ah Paw told Eileen Yin-Fei Lo it was important to know how to cook so if she were rich, servants wouldn't be able to <u>take advantage of</u> her.

   _____

   b. Slow Food advocates work to <u>do away with</u> the "nuke it and eat it" American lifestyle. _____

   c. The smell of food coming from the kitchen caused Marco to <u>think back on</u> the dishes his mother used to cook when he was a child.

   _____

   d. Before you start cooking, you should <u>look over</u> the recipe to make sure you understand it and have all the ingredients. _____

4. flip   appear   lower   start

   a. Don't forget to <u>turn over</u> the fish before it burns. _____

   b. If you don't <u>turn</u> the heat <u>down</u>, the meat will burn.

   _____

   c. I'm going to <u>turn on</u> the television to watch the cooking show.

   _____

   d. Although a few years ago they weren't so popular, fast-food restaurants are beginning to <u>turn up</u> all over the world. _____

3 *Complete the paragraphs with phrasal verbs from exercise 2 on pages 181–182 and the grammar box on pages 183–184 in place of the verbs in parentheses. Be sure to use the correct tense.*

When I am asked to (*remember*) **1.** _____ the best meal I ever had, it is easy for me to (*imagine*) **2.** _____ it. It was in Paris, on the Left Bank. I must have been in my early twenties, traveling with my friends. We were always broke and, as a result, we ate a lot of hot dogs and street food. Even so, we thought we lived like kings. One day we thought we should splurge for dinner and actually eat in a sit-down restaurant. Of course, having very little money, we had to be careful where we ate: not too expensive, yet still with splendidly delicious food. This demanded that we spend the day (*examining*) **3.** _____ the menus of every restaurant on the Left Bank before committing to the perfect one. Finally we found it. We knew it was perfect before we even (*entered*) **4.** _____ it. It was a lovely little Algerian place with all the couscous[1] you could eat! We were very hungry, so we knew we had to (*exploit*) **5.** _____ this opportunity.

We returned that night, freshly showered and dressed for our night out. As soon as we sat down, delicious French bread was served with tall glasses of ice cold water with lemon. We ordered. While we waited, the waiter (*appeared*) **6.** _____ with appetizers that we were told the cook sent out for us because we looked so hungry. At the very moment we finished our appetizers, the main course arrived. It was splendid! An enormous silver bowl of couscous and chicken was placed in the middle of the table with a large silver ladle, like a spoon. We served ourselves and ate and ate. As soon as we finished, the waiter removed the bowl . . . and replaced it with another! After that meal, we did not just think we were kings, we knew it! We stumbled back to our hotel, deliriously happy, with full stomachs and wonderful memories.

---

[1] *couscous:* semolina wheat

B STYLE: Narrative Voice

1 *Examine the following excerpt from "The Chinese Kitchen" and discuss the questions with the class.*

Food is not only life-giving but also a source of familial or societal leanings. Our food is inextricably linked with manners, with form, with tradition, with history. I grew up with these beliefs. I remember my father, Lo Pak Wan, my first cooking teacher, telling me that we must eat our food first with our eyes, then with our minds, then with our noses, and finally with our mouths. He believed this. He taught this to my brother and me.

1. What is the topic of Eileen Yin-Fei Lo's writing? What is the controlling idea? Why do you think she has chosen to share her story?

2. How does Yin-Fei Lo illustrate or support her idea? Does she use facts, statistics, or personal experiences? Is this effective? Why or why not?

NOTE: see Unit 1, Style: Topic Sentences, pages 18–19, for explanation of topic, main idea, controlling idea, and supporting ideas.

Narrative Voice

A **narrative** is a writing style that uses events, memories, and personal experiences to illustrate a story. It is an effective style to use when a personal experience deeply influenced you or caused you to think differently. Eileen Yin-Fei Lo's writing is a narrative that describes her experiences growing up in a Chinese kitchen and how these experiences influenced her. She illustrates her story using memories of her father, mother, and grandmother.

Writing a Narrative

There are many different ways to make your narrative interesting and fun to read. You can use different characters with different perspectives to illustrate your controlling idea. You can also vary your sentence structure to make the reading flow nicely.

Note that although most narratives are written in the first person using *I*, the third person (*he, she, it*) can also be used.

Using Different Perspectives

Usually a narrative is written from one viewpoint, that of the author, but in "The Chinese Kitchen," Yin-Fei Lo also uses the viewpoints of her mother, her father, and her grandmother. By choosing these characters to illustrate her story, she brings alive the idea that food, family, and society are linked. Introducing different characters with different perspectives is an interesting way to support your controlling idea.

(continued)

Using a Variety of Sentence Lengths

When you write a narrative, don't write only long sentences or short sentences. Try to use a variety of sentence lengths. A combination of long and short sentences creates a lively feeling to your writing. Note the different sentence lengths in this excerpt:

I am tempted to suggest that she was a brilliant, instinctive kitchen chemist. I will say it. Brilliant she was indeed, her knowledge about foods was encyclopedic, and she was never wrong about cooking, then or now, in my memory.

Using Parallel Structure

You can create a pleasing rhythm to your narrative by repeating patterns of words, phrases, or clauses with the same grammatical structure. Use these structures in one sentence separated by commas. For example, Yin-Fei Lo writes:

*Our food is inextricably linked **with** manners, **with** form, **with** tradition, **with** history.*

Using Quoted (Direct) Speech

Quoted speech, or stating someone's exact words, is often used in narratives. With quoted speech you relay exactly what the speaker said, using quotation marks. For example:

"Clean it," Ah Paw would say when I had finished. "If you do not, the food you chop next will not stick together."

Organizing Your Narrative

Writing a narrative is like telling a good story. It must be well-organized and interesting in order to keep the reader engaged. In order to write an effective narrative, keep these points in mind:

1. **Have a clear topic and controlling idea.** Think about the event (the topic) and why this is a story worth telling (the controlling idea). The controlling idea answers the question: Why do you want to share this story? What new insight or awareness did you gain from the event?

2. **Support your controlling idea throughout your writing.** Use examples and details to support and enhance your controlling idea. Make sure they directly relate to the controlling idea.

3. **Use a chronological sequence.** Use time sequence words to explain the order in which events occur. For example use *first, next, then,* and *afterwards.*

2 *Answer the following questions about the narrative techniques used in Reading One. Share your answers with a partner.*

1. Where does Eileen Yin-Fei Lo state the topic and controlling idea of her story?

2. Does she support her controlling idea throughout the story with strong examples and details? Does the support explain and enhance the controlling idea? What is an example of an effective support she uses?

3. Does she use a chronological sequence to describe a particular experience? Where and how does she use it?

4. Does she use quoted speech? What are some places in the story where she uses quoted speech most effectively?

5. Does she use a variety of sentence lengths? Look at the first paragraph and underline examples of both long and short sentences.

6. Does she use parallel structure? Look at the first paragraph and underline examples of parallel structure.

3 *Eileen Yin-Fei Lo states that food is linked with tradition and history. Think of a food tradition from your culture which is associated with a holiday, religion, or family tradition. Write a narrative paragraph describing the tradition. After you have finished, exchange paragraphs with a partner. Answer the questions below about your partner's paragraph.*

1. What is the topic and controlling idea?

   _____

   _____

2. Does the writer support the controlling idea throughout the story with strong examples and details? What is the most effective support used?

   _____

   _____

3. Does the author describe any events using a chronological sequence? Give an example.

   _____

   _____

4. Does the author use quoted speech? What are some of the places in the story where quoted speech is used most effectively?

   _____

   _____

5. Does the author use a variety of sentences lengths? Give an example.

_____

_____

6. Does the author use parallel structure? Give an example.

_____

_____

7. What part of the narrative did you like best? Why?

_____

_____

C   WRITING TOPICS

Write an essay about one of these topics. Be sure to use the ideas, vocabulary, grammar, and style that you have learned in this unit.

1. The Slow Food movement suggests that you go to restaurants that specialize in local, regional cuisine. They state, "When traveling, eat what and where the locals eat." Do you follow this advice? Write about a memorable meal that you ate while traveling.

2. The smells of certain foods can often trigger a strong memory or moment from the past. Are there any food smells that trigger a specific memory or feeling for you? What are they? What do you think of when you smell them?

3. Think about the expression "you are what you eat" and apply it to yourself. Choose one of your favorite foods or food traditions and discuss how it reflects who you are.

4. Look back at the statistics in Preparing to Read on pages 168–169. Keeping these statistics in mind, answer the following questions: Has fast food changed the way you eat or the way your culture eats? How?

D   RESEARCH TOPIC

Interview a friend or relative about his or her most memorable meal. Use the following outline to take notes during the interview. Then, write the person's information as a narrative. Share it with your class.

Person interviewed:

Month/Year of the meal:

Location of the meal (include city and country, home, restaurant, or other):

Reason for the meal (special holiday, birthday, or no specific reason):

People the meal was shared with:

Description of the meal (include look, taste, touch, smell):

Information about preparation (how the meal was prepared):

Interesting events that happened at the meal:

Why the meal was so memorable:

For step-by-step practice in the writing process, see the *Writing Activity Book, High Intermediate,* Unit 8.

Assignment	Narrative essay
Prewriting	Listing in order
Organizing	Sequencing events in a narrative
Revising	Using different perspectives
	Using phrasal verbs
Editing	Developing sentence variety

For Unit 8 Internet activities, visit the NorthStar Companion Website at
http://www.longman.com/northstar

The Grass Is Always Greener

Jamaica Kincaid
Born: Antigua,[1] 1949
Occupation: Writer
Immigrated to the U.S. in 1966

Arnold Schwarzenegger
Born: Graz, Austria, 1947
Occupation: Actor
Immigrated to the U.S. in 1968

Gloria Estefan
Born: Havana, Cuba, 1957
Occupation: Singer
Immigrated to the U.S. in 1959

1 Focus on the Topic

A PREDICTING

Look at the photographs and the title of the unit. Then discuss these questions with a partner.

1. What do these people have in common?

2. What personal history do you think they share?

3. What do you think the title of the unit means? What do you think this unit will be about?

---

[1] *Antigua:* an island in the Caribbean

B   SHARING INFORMATION

Work in a small group. Brainstorm a list of reasons why people immigrate. Think about economic, political, and personal reasons. Complete the chart with as many reasons as you can and discuss your reasons with the class. If you wish, share any personal experiences you have had.

ECONOMIC REASONS	POLITICAL REASONS	PERSONAL REASONS

C   PREPARING TO READ

BACKGROUND

The story you are about to read is from the novel *Lucy* by Jamaica Kincaid. Jamaica Kincaid was only 16 years old when she left her home in Antigua to come to New York. She worked in the home of an American family as a nanny, taking care of the children. After working at several domestic jobs,[1] in and around New York, Kincaid entered college and eventually began writing for *The New Yorker* magazine. She became a highly successful and respected author. She has written many short stories about her native island and her family.

Imagine you are 16 years old and have left your home on a tropical island. This is your first time away from the island and your family. You arrive in New York in the wintertime. What problems do you think you will face? Think about the differences you will find in the food, climate, and living conditions.

Write down your ideas and share them with a partner.

_____

_____

_____

_____

[1] *domestic job:* a job in which you work in a home cleaning, cooking, or taking care of children

VOCABULARY FOR COMPREHENSION

Work with a partner. All of the underlined words have two meanings. Circle the letter of the meaning as it is used in the sentence. This is the meaning of the word as it is used in Reading One.

1. <u>Bouts</u> with one's enemies rarely end peacefully.
   a. fights or contests between two opponents
   b. periods of time spent in a particular way

2. The community center has been a <u>fixture</u> in my neighborhood for 25 years.
   a. something that is always present and not likely to move
   b. a piece of equipment, such as an electric light, that is attached to a home

3. I was no longer in a tropical zone and I felt cold inside and out, the first time such a <u>sensation</u> had come over me.
   a. big event causing great excitement
   b. feeling or emotion

4. We sat on the <u>bank</u> and watched the sunset while eating our picnic.
   a. a business that keeps and lends money
   b. land along the side of a river or lake

5. Agatha Christie's books have sold millions of copies around the world because her stories always have great <u>plots</u>.
   a. pieces of land
   b. actions that form a story

6. After living abroad for many months, she began to <u>long</u> for her mother's cooking.
   a. relatively great distance
   b. desire or want very much

7. The child became bored and started to <u>twist</u> in his chair during the long movie.
   a. change the true meaning of something
   b. turn or bend part of the body

8. The Statue of Liberty is probably the most famous <u>sight</u> in New York City.
   a. ability to see very clearly
   b. something unusual or interesting to see

9. He was in a state of <u>rage</u> after his airline tickets and travelers checks were stolen.
   a. extreme anger
   b. popular trend or fad

10. He thought it was going to rain, but wasn't sure because he could see a small <u>patch</u> of blue sky in the distance.
    a. area
    b. bandage

2 Focus on Reading

Read the first paragraph. Write short answers to the following questions. Share your answers with a partner. Then read the rest of the story.

1. Which words tell you about Lucy's emotions on her first day in New York?

   _____

   _____

2. What do you think will happen? What do you think the author will describe in the rest of the story?

   _____

   _____

POOR VISITOR

BY JAMAICA KINCAID
(from *Lucy*)

1   It was my first day. I had come the night before, a gray-black and cold night before—as it was to be in the middle of January, though I didn't know that at the time—and I could not see anything clearly on the way in from the airport, even though there were lights everywhere. As we drove along, someone would single out[1] to me a famous building, an important street, a park, a bridge, that when built was thought to be a spectacle.[2] In a daydream I used to have, all these places were points of happiness to me; all these places were lifeboats to my small drowning soul, for I would imagine myself entering and leaving them, and just that—entering and leaving over and over again—would see me through a bad feeling I did not have a name for. I only knew it felt a little like sadness but heavier than that. Now that I saw these places, they looked ordinary, dirty, worn down by so many people entering and leaving them in real life, and it occurred to me that I could not be the only person in the world for whom they were a fixture of fantasy. It was not my first bout with the disappointment of reality and it would not be my last. The

[1] *single out:* to point out, show
[2] *spectacle:* something remarkable or impressive

undergarments that I wore were all new, bought for my journey, and as I sat in the car, twisting this way and that to get a good view of the sights before me, I was reminded of how uncomfortable the new can make you feel.

2   I got in an elevator, something I had never done before, and then I was in an apartment and seated at a table eating food just taken from a refrigerator. In the place I had just come from, I always lived in a house, and my house did not have a refrigerator in it. Everything I was experiencing— the ride in the elevator, being in an apartment, eating day-old food that had been stored in a refrigerator—was such a good

idea that I could imagine I would grow used to it and like it very much, but at first it was all so new that I had to smile with my mouth turned down at the corners. I slept soundly that night, but it wasn't because I was happy and comfortable—quite the opposite; it was because I didn't want to take in anything else.

3   That morning, the morning of my first day, the morning that followed my first night, was a sunny morning. It was not the sort of bright-yellow sun making everything curl at the edges, almost in fright, that I was used to, but a pale-yellow sun, as if the sun had grown weak from trying too hard to shine; but still it was sunny, and that was nice and made me miss my home less. And so, seeing the sun, I got up and put on a dress, a gay³ dress made out of madras cloth—the same sort of dress that I would wear if I were at home and setting out for a day in the country. It was all wrong. The sun was shining but the air was cold. It was the middle of January, after all. But I did not know that the sun could shine and the air remain cold; no one had ever told me. What a feeling that was! How can I explain? Something I had always known— the way I knew my skin was the color brown of a nut rubbed repeatedly with a soft cloth, or the way I knew my own name—something I took completely for granted, "the sun is shining, the air is warm," was not so. I was no longer in a tropical zone, and this realization now entered my life like a flow of water dividing formerly dry and solid ground, creating two banks, one of which was my past—so familiar and predictable that even my unhappiness then made me happy now just to think of it—the other my future, a gray blank, an overcast

³ *gay:* cheerful; happy

seascape on which rain was falling and no boats were in sight. I was no longer in a tropical zone and I felt cold inside and out, the first time such a sensation had come over me.

4   In books I had read—from time to time, when the plot called for it— someone would suffer from homesickness. A person would leave a not so very nice situation and go somewhere else, somewhere a lot better, and then long to go back where it was not very nice. How impatient I would become with such a person, for I would feel that I was in a not so nice situation myself, and how I wanted to go somewhere else. But now I, too, felt that I wanted to be back where I came from. I understood it, I knew where I stood there. If I had had to draw a picture of my future then, it would have been a large gray patch surrounded by black, blacker, blackest.

5   What a surprise this was to me, that I longed to be back in the place that I came from, that I longed to sleep in a bed I had outgrown, that I longed to be with the people whose smallest, most natural gesture would call up in me such a rage that I longed to see them all dead at my feet. Oh, I had imagined that with my one swift act—leaving home and coming to this new place—I could leave behind me, as if it were an old garment⁴ never to be worn again, my sad thoughts, my sad feelings, and my discontent with life in general as it presented itself to me. In the past, the thought of being in my present situation had been a comfort, but now I did not even have this to look forward to, and so I lay down on my bed and dreamt I was eating a bowl of pink mullet⁵ and green figs cooked in coconut milk, and it had been cooked by my grandmother, which was why the taste of it pleased me so, for she was the person I liked best in the world and those were the things I liked best to eat also.

⁴ **garment:** a piece of clothing
⁵ **pink mullet:** a type of fish

READING FOR MAIN IDEAS

*Write true (**T**) or false (**F**) for each sentence. If the statement is false, correct it. Write the number of the paragraph that supports your answer.*

Paragraph

_____   1. Lucy feels very comfortable in the new country.   _____

_____

_____   2. Lucy finds everything very much the same as she expected   _____
and very similar to her own country.

_____

_____   3. Lucy is unsure of her future.   _____

_____

_____ 4. Lucy was a happy young girl in her home country.   _____

_____

_____ 5. Lucy is surprised that she is homesick.   _____

_____

_____ 6. Lucy's dreams became reality in the new country.   _____

_____

READING FOR DETAILS

Imagine that Lucy wrote the following letter to her grandmother. In it she describes her new life in the United States. The letter has eight factual errors. Read it and underline the errors. Write the corrections above the errors. Explain the incorrect information by referring to the story. Discuss with a partner.

Dear Grandmother,

I had a wonderful trip. The weather was warm and sunny, and I loved traveling by boat. Driving through the city, I saw many of the famous sights that I had dreamt about before my trip. They were beautiful.

The apartment building where I am staying has an elevator. As you know, I had never seen one before, much less been in one! It's great not to have to walk up the stairs. The apartment is furnished and it has a brand new refrigerator, just like the one we have at home.

After a good night's sleep, I awoke to another bright, sunny day. I put on a pretty summer dress. It was just the right thing. Despite the warm weather, I felt a feeling of homesickness coming over me. It's hard to explain why this would happen, but it did. Perhaps it has to do with the insecurity I feel about my future.

If you had told me before I left that I would miss my life back home, I wouldn't have believed you. Nevertheless, that is what has happened. Don't worry about me, I'll be fine. I'll write again as soon as I have more to tell you.

Love,

Lucy

P.S. I enjoyed eating the pink mullet and green figs that you cooked for me to eat on my trip. It made me feel less homesick.

REACTING TO THE READING

1 *Work with a partner. Read the following sentences from "Poor Visitor" and answer the questions. Share your answers with the class.*

1. "In a daydream I used to have, all these places were points of happiness to me; all these places were lifeboats to my small drowning soul."

   What does Lucy mean by "lifeboats to my small drowning soul"?

   _____

   _____

2. "I was reminded of how uncomfortable the new can make you feel."

   What does Lucy mean by this?

   _____

   _____

3. "But at first it was all so new that I had to smile with my mouth turned down at the corners."

   Why does Lucy smile with her mouth turned down?

   _____

   _____

4. "But now I, too, felt that I wanted to be back where I came from. I understood it, I knew where I stood there."

   Why does Lucy want to be back in her home country?

   _____

   _____

5. "Oh, I had imagined that with my one swift act—leaving home and coming to this new place—I could leave behind me, as if it were an old garment never to be worn again, my sad thoughts, my sad feelings, and my discontent with life in general as it presented itself to me."

   What does Lucy realize about herself and her feelings?

   _____

   _____

2 *Work with a partner. Read the following sentences from "Poor Visitor." Have you experienced these feelings? When? What happened? Share your experiences with your partner.*

1. "Now that I saw these places, they looked dirty, worn down. . . . It was not my first bout with the disappointment of reality."

2. "I was reminded of how uncomfortable the new can make you feel."

3. "I slept soundly that night, but it wasn't because I was happy and comfortable—quite the opposite; it was because I didn't want to take in anything else."

4. "Something I had always known . . . something I took completely for granted . . . was not so."

5. "But now I, too, felt that I wanted to be back where I came from. I understood it, I knew where I stood there."

B READING TWO: *Nostalgia*

This poem was written by a Puerto Rican* poet who describes his nostalgia for his homeland. Nostalgia is the feeling you get when you long for something good from your past. For example, many people have feelings of nostalgia for their childhood.

Read the first stanza (group of lines) of the poem and answer the following questions. Then read the rest of the poem.

1. What do you think "this country" is?

2. How does he compare this country and his home country?

---

* Although Puerto Rico is a commonwealth of the United States, there are many cultural differences between the mainland United States and the island of Puerto Rico.

Nostalgia

BY VIRGILIO DÁVILA (1869–1943)

1 "Mamma, Borinquen[1] calls me,
   this country is not mine,
   Borinquen is pure flame
   and here I am dying of the cold."

2 In search of a better future
   I left the native home,
   and established my store
   in the middle of New York.
   What I see around me
   is a sad panorama,[2]
   and my spirit calls out,
   wounded by much nostalgia,
   for the return to the home nest,
   Mamma, Borinquen calls me!

3 Where will I find here
   like in my criollo[3] land
   a dish of chicken and rice,
   a cup of good coffee?
   Where, oh where will I see
   radiant in their attire
   the girls, rich in vigor,
   whose glances bedazzle?[4]
   Here eyes do not bedazzle,
   this country is not mine!

4 If I listen to a song here
   of those I learned at home,
   or a danza[5] by Tavarez,
   Campos, or Dueño Colon,
   my sensitive heart
   is more enflamed with patriotic love,

---

[1] **Borinquen:** the name the people of Puerto Rico use when referring to their homeland; the Borinquen Indians, or Boriqueños, were the original inhabitants of Puerto Rico
[2] **panorama:** a view, scene, sight
[3] **criollo:** Spanish-American
[4] **bedazzle:** to impress, enchant
[5] **danza:** a type of dance music from the nineteenth century

and a herald[6] that faithful proclaims
this holy feeling
the wail "Borinquen is pure flame!"
comes to my ears.

5 In my land, what beauty!
In the hardest winter
not a tree is seen bare,
not a vale[7] without green.
The flower rules the garden,
the river meanders talkative,
the bird in the shadowy wood
sings his arbitrary[8] song,
and here . . . The snow is a shroud,[9]
here I am dying of the cold.

[6] *herald:* messenger
[7] *vale:* a valley
[8] *arbitrary:* something random
[9] *shroud:* a covering or burial garment

Answer the following questions. Then share your answers with the class.

1. What does Virgilio Dávila miss about his native country? List at least four things he misses.

    1. _____

    2. _____

    3. _____

    4. _____

2. Are these things similar to or different from the things you said you miss (or would miss) in exercise 2 on page 201? Explain.

    _____

    _____

    _____

    _____

C   LINKING READINGS ONE AND TWO

1 *There are several similar themes or topics described in both readings. Complete the chart with three more themes and an example of each from the readings. Discuss your answers with a partner.*

THEME	EXAMPLE FROM READING ONE	EXAMPLE FROM READING TWO
1. *weather*		
2.		
3.		
4.		

2 *Both Lucy and Virgilio Dávila feel very strongly about their home countries and their adopted country. What word(s) do you think Lucy and Virgilio Dávila would use to describe their home countries? What word(s) would they use to describe their adopted country (United States)?*

Lucy (Antigua) _____

   (United States) _____

Virgilio Dávila (Puerto Rico) _____

   (United States) _____

3 Focus on Vocabulary

1 *Complete the chart using words from the box below. Decide whether each word is associated with the author's home country or adopted country. If necessary, refer back to the readings.*

bad	dirty	new	shadowy	warm
bare	dry	ordinary	shroud	weak
beauty	~~flame~~	overcast	solid	~~winter~~
bedazzle	gay	radiant	uncomfortable	worn down
cold	gray-black	sad	vigor	

HOME COUNTRY	ADOPTED COUNTRY
flame	*winter*

Work with a partner. Discuss what the words in each column have in common. Why do you think the authors chose these words to describe their feelings? Explain.

2 *Read this information about analogies.*

As explained in Unit 3, page 58, analogies are comparisons between two words that seem similar or are related in some way. For example, in item 1, *warm* and *cold* are opposites; in the same way, *sunny* and *overcast* are opposites.

Work with a partner. Discuss the relationship between the words. Circle the letter of the word that best completes each analogy.

1. warm : cold :: sunny : _____
     a. light   **b.** overcast   **c.** vigorous

2. flame : light :: drowning : _____
     a. feeling   **b.** dying   **c.** crying

3. spectacles : sights :: happy : _____
   a. gay   **b.** uncomfortable   **c.** shadowy

4. beauty : bedazzles :: nostalgia : _____
   a. rules   **b.** frightens   **c.** saddens

5. feeling : sensation :: covering : _____
   a. undergarment   **b.** daydream   **c.** shroud

6. fantasy : reality :: arbitrary : _____
   a. predictable   **b.** happy   **c.** rainy

7. radiant : bedazzling :: worn down : _____
   a. gay   **b.** old and tired   **c.** black

3 *Imagine you are either Lucy's grandmother in Antigua or a relative of Virgilio Dávila's in Puerto Rico. Write a letter to Lucy or Virgilio. Respond to what they have written, and be sure to address their homesickness. Use 10–12 words and phrases from exercises 1 and 2 on pages 205–206.*

4 Focus on Writing

A GRAMMAR: Past Perfect

1 *Examine the following sentences, and discuss the questions with a partner.*

   a. By the time Lucy arrived in New York, she <u>had</u> already <u>imagined</u> what New York would look like.

   b. Lucy <u>had</u> just <u>put</u> on her summer dress when she realized it was cold outside.

   c. Before Lucy moved to New York, she <u>had longed</u> to go there.

1. In sentence *a*, did Lucy arrive in New York first, or did she imagine what New York looked like first?

2. In sentence *b*, did Lucy realize it was cold outside before she put on her summer dress?

3. In sentence *c*, which happened first—Lucy's move to New York or her longing to go there?

4. What helped you decide the order of events in these sentences?

Past Perfect

The **past perfect** form of a verb is used to show that something happened before a specific time or event in the past.

Forming the Past Perfect

- The past perfect is formed with *had* + **past participle**.

  Lucy **had** never **been** in an elevator before.

Past Perfect and a Specific Time or Event in the Past

- To show that something happened before a specific time in the past, use the past perfect with *by* + a certain time in the past.

  By the next morning, Lucy **had become** very homesick.

Past Perfect with Two Past Events

- When talking about two events that happened in the past, use the past perfect to show the event that happened first (the earlier event). The simple past is often used to show the second event. In other words, the event in the past perfect happened before the event in the simple past.

- Time words such as *after* and *as soon as* are used to introduce the first event (past perfect).

  As soon as she **had put on** her summer dress, she had a strange sensation.

- *Before* and *by the time* are used to introduce the second event (simple past).

  Lucy **had lived** with her grandmother **before** she moved to New York. (First she lived with her grandmother. Then she moved to New York.)

- *When* can be used to introduce either the first or the second event. Notice the difference.

  Lucy **had put on** her dress **when** she realized the weather was cold. (First she put on her dress. Then she realized the weather was cold.)

  Lucy **put on** her dress **when** she realized the weather was cold. (First she realized the weather was cold. Then she put on her dress.)

- *Already, never,* and *ever* are often used with the past perfect to emphasize the event that happened first.

  Lucy **had never eaten** food from a refrigerator before then.

  No one **had ever told** Lucy that the sun could shine and the air remain cold.

GRAMMAR TIP: When a sentence begins with a dependent clause (the clause beginning with a time word), a comma separates it from the main clause. When a sentence begins with the main clause, no comma is necessary.

2 *Each of the following sentences talks about two events which happened in the past. The individual events are listed below each sentence. In what order did the events happen? Write **1** for the first event and **2** for the second event.*

1. By the time Lucy arrived in New York, she had already imagined what New York would look like.

   _2_ Lucy arrived in New York.

   _1_ Lucy imagined what New York looked like.

2. Before Dávila established his store in New York, he had lived in Puerto Rico.

   _____ Dávila established his store in New York.

   _____ Dávila lived in Puerto Rico.

3. The immigrants had already seen the Statue of Liberty when Ellis Island came into view.

   _____ The immigrants saw the Statue of Liberty.

   _____ Ellis Island came into view.

4. Dávila had never felt so alone before he moved to New York.

   _____ Dávila moved to New York.

   _____ Dávila never felt so alone.

5. After Lucy had woken up, she put on a gay summer dress.

   _____ Lucy woke up.

   _____ Lucy put on a gay summer dress.

6. The immigrants had never studied a second language before they moved to the new country.

   _____ The immigrants never studied a second language.

   _____ The immigrants moved to a new country.

7. By the time Dávila established his store in New York, he had grown very nostalgic for his homeland.

   _____ Dávila was nostalgic for his homeland.

   _____ Dávila established his store in New York.

8. As soon as Jamaica Kincaid had moved from Antigua to New York, she needed to find a job and a place to stay.

   _____ Jamaica Kincaid moved from Antigua to New York.

   _____ She needed to find a job and a place to stay.

3 *Use Jamaica Kincaid's time line to complete the sentences that follow. Use the past perfect or the simple past tenses. Use events close to the time of the event mentioned.*

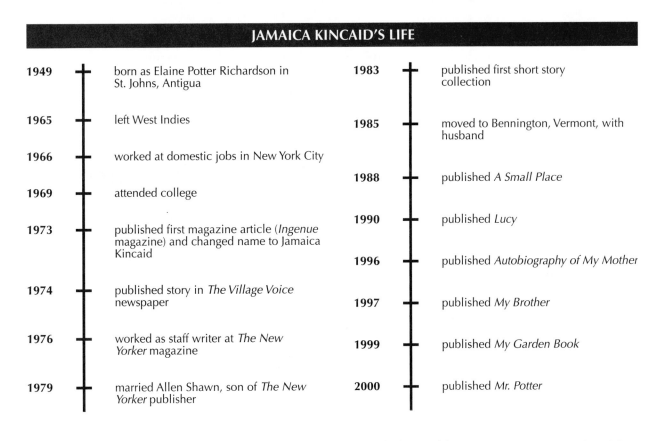

	JAMAICA KINCAID'S LIFE		
1949	born as Elaine Potter Richardson in St. Johns, Antigua	1983	published first short story collection
1965	left West Indies	1985	moved to Bennington, Vermont, with husband
1966	worked at domestic jobs in New York City	1988	published *A Small Place*
1969	attended college	1990	published *Lucy*
1973	published first magazine article (*Ingenue* magazine) and changed name to Jamaica Kincaid	1996	published *Autobiography of My Mother*
1974	published story in *The Village Voice* newspaper	1997	published *My Brother*
1976	worked as staff writer at *The New Yorker* magazine	1999	published *My Garden Book*
1979	married Allen Shawn, son of *The New Yorker* publisher	2000	published *Mr. Potter*

1. After Elaine Potter Richardson had changed her name to Jamaica Kincaid,
   she published a story in the Village Voice. _____

2. By the time she published *Autobiography of My Mother*, _____
   _____

3. Jamaica Kincaid had moved to Bennington, Vermont, before _____
   _____

4. As soon as _____ ,
   she found a domestic job in New York.

5. By 1976, _____
   _____

6. She had already worked as a staff writer at *The New Yorker* magazine when

_____

7. After _____,

she worked as a staff writer at *The New Yorker* magazine.

8. She had already attended college before _____

_____

B   STYLE: Comparisons and Contrasts

1 *Examine the paragraph, and discuss the questions with a partner.*

Lucy faces many changes upon her arrival in New York City. First she is struck with the change in climate. Her native climate is warm and the sun is brilliant <u>while</u> New York in January is very cold and the sun is lifeless. Her living conditions are different, too. In New York she lives in an apartment building. <u>In contrast</u>, she lived in a house in her native country. In addition, she finds herself eating food that has just been taken from the refrigerator <u>whereas</u> she always ate her grandmother's freshly cooked meals in her homeland. Other aspects of her life remain the same. Lucy faces many different problems and issues in New York <u>in the same way</u> she did in Antigua. She has learned that she cannot leave her troubles behind like clothes she has outgrown.

1. Look at the underlined words. Which words introduce ideas that are similar? Which words introduce ideas that are different?

2. Four topics are compared and contrasted in this paragraph. What are they?

Comparisons and Contrasts

Comparisons point out ideas that are similar. **Contrasts** point out ideas that are different.

Subordinating Conjunctions

Subordinating conjunctions are used to contrast the ideas in two clauses. They join the independent clause to the dependent clause being contrasted. Examples of subordinating conjunctions include *while* and *whereas*. Note that these words do not introduce a complete thought. They introduce dependent clauses. The independent clause usually describes the point that is being emphasized or is more important.

Her native climate is warm and the sun is brilliant **while** New York in January is very cold and the sun is lifeless.

More emphasis: The weather in her native country is warm.
Less emphasis: The weather in New York is cold.

Whereas the sun in New York is lifeless, the sun in her native country is brilliant.

Less emphasis: The sun in New York is lifeless.
More emphasis: The sun in her native country is brilliant.

Punctuation

See the Grammar Tip on page 207. The same punctuation rules apply for dependent and independent clauses.

Transitions

- Transitions show the connection between two independent clauses (two sentences).

Transitions for comparisons include:	**Transitions for contrasts include:**
similarly	in contrast
in the same way	on the other hand
likewise	however

- Two independent clauses can be combined in one sentence by using a semicolon (;) and a comma (,):

In New York she lives in an apartment building; **however**, she lived in a house in her native country.

- The two independent clauses can also be written as separate sentences:

In New York she lives in an apartment building. **However**, she lived in a house in her native country.

- Two independent clauses can also be combined as a simple sentence using the phrase *in the same way*.

Lucy came to New York in search of a better future **in the same way** Dávila did.

2 *Combine the following pairs of sentences to make comparisons and contrasts. Use the boldfaced words or phrases given.*

1. likewise

    a. Lucy feels homesick.

    b. Dávila feels nostalgic.

    Lucy feels homesick; likewise, Dávila feels nostalgic.

2. in the same way

    a. Dávila dislikes harsh winter with its bare trees.

    b. Lucy dislikes the pale winter sun.

    _____

3. similarly

    a. Lucy misses her grandmother's home cooking.

    b. Dávila misses his country's native food.

    _____

4. on the other hand

    a. Dávila opened his own store in New York.

    b. Lucy worked for a family as a nanny.

    _____

5. in contrast

    a. Lucy is a young woman.

    b. Dávila is an older man.

    _____

6. while

    a. "Poor Visitor" was written in the last half of the twentieth century.

    b. "Nostalgia" was written in the first half of the twentieth century.

    _____

7. **whereas**

   a. Dávila misses his culture.

   b. Lucy misses her family.

   _____

8. **however**

   a. Jamaica Kincaid was born in Antigua.

   b. Dávila was born in Puerto Rico.

   _____

3 _Complete the chart comparing Dávila's life in Puerto Rico and in New York. Use the list from the Reading Two column in the chart on page 204 as a guide. Then use the information from the chart below to write complete sentences._

PUERTO RICO		NEW YORK
1. _The weather is hot and sunny._	whereas	**1.** _The weather is cold and snowy._
2.	however	**2.**
3.	in contrast	**3.**
4.	on the other hand	**4.**

1. _The weather in Puerto Rico is hot and sunny whereas it is cold and snowy in New York._ _____

2. _____

   _____

3. _____

   _____

4. _____

   _____

C WRITING TOPICS

Write an essay about one of these topics. Be sure to use some of the some of the ideas, vocabulary, grammar, and style that you have learned in this unit.

1. "Poor Visitor" and "Nostalgia" have many similar themes. Compare the themes, using specific examples from the two readings. Refer to the chart in Linking Readings One and Two, exercise 1, on page 204 if you need help.

2. Have you ever left your home country to live in another country? What were your feelings about your home country when you first arrived in the new country? What feelings did you have after being away for a while? Did you experience any bouts of nostalgia? If so, what did you do to overcome it?

3. "Living in another language means growing another self, and it takes time for that other self to become familiar."

—Allistair Reed

Discuss the meaning of this quote and how it applies to you and your experiences. Has studying English changed your life? If so, how? What is different about you now, since studying English? Are these positive or negative changes?

D RESEARCH TOPIC

Report on U.S. immigrants.

Step 1: Work in a small group. Look at the list of famous U.S. immigrants on the next page. Brainstorm a list of other famous or not so famous immigrants (relatives, friends, an acquaintance from your neighborhood or school). Write as much information as you know about them—for example, occupation, country of origin, country of immigration, and reasons for immigrating.

Step 2: Choose an immigrant you would like to learn more about. You can choose someone from your brainstorming list or from the list below. If you choose someone you know, arrange a personal interview. If you choose someone famous, research this person at the library or on the Internet. Write a report including answers to the following questions. Present your report to the class.

1. Who is the person?

2. Where was the person born?

3. Where did the person immigrate to?

4. How old was the person when he or she immigrated?

5. Why did this person immigrate?

6. How long has the person been living in the new country?

7. What other personal information did you find?

Some Famous U.S. Immigrants

Politicians
Madeleine Albright, former U.S. Secretary of State (Czech Republic)
Henry Kissinger, former U.S. Secretary of State (Germany)
Elaine Chao, U.S. Secretary of Labor (Taiwan)

Authors
Jamaica Kincaid (Antigua)
Isabel Allende (Chile)
Frank McCourt (Ireland)

Musicians
Carlos Santana, rock guitarist (Mexico)
Plácido Domingo, opera singer (Spain)
Yo Yo Ma, cellist (France)
Midori, classical violinist (Japan)
Itzhak Perlman, violinist (Israel)
Andrés Segovia, classical guitarist (Spain)
Elton John, singer/composer (England)

Actors
Andy Garcia (Cuba)
Audrey Hepburn (Belgium)
Iman (Somalia)
Michael J. Fox (Canada)

Athletes
Martina Navratilova, retired tennis player (Czech Republic)
Sammy Sosa, baseball player (Dominican Republic)
Hakeem Olajuwon, basketball player (Nigeria)
Wayne Gretzky, retired hockey player (Canada)
Nadia Comaneci, gymnast (Romania)

Other People
George Soros, philanthropist (Hungary)
Albert Einstein, physicist (Germany)
Oscar de la Renta, fashion designer (Dominican Republic)

For step-by-step practice in the writing process, see the *Writing Activity Book, High Intermediate*, Unit 9.

Assignment	Comparison and contrast essay
Prewriting	Charting
Organizing	Comparing and contrasting
Revising	Using transitions to compare and contrast
	Showing the relationship between events with the past perfect
Editing	Punctuating dependent and independent clauses

For Unit 9 Internet activities, visit the NorthStar Companion Website at http://www.longman.com/northstar

Take It or Leave It

who needs all this **technology** anyway?!

I wish it would all go away!!! microprocessors... microwaves... frozen corn on the cob... operating systems named BOB.

well o.k... maybe a little technology.

©1998 Bill Layne

1 Focus on the Topic

A PREDICTING

Look at the cartoon and the title of the unit. Then discuss these questions with a partner.

1. How do you think the character in the cartoon feels about technology?

2. Are these feelings similar to or different from your own feelings about technology? Explain your answer.

3. What do you think the title of the unit means? What would be the consequences of your taking—or leaving—technology?

B   SHARING INFORMATION

Check (✓) whether you feel the technology listed is a necessity or a luxury. Add anything you feel is missing from the list. Compare your opinions in a small group.

TECHNOLOGY	NECESSITY	LUXURY
electricity		
running water		
washing machine/dryer		
automatic dishwasher		
microwave		
motion sensor lights[1]		
automatic garage-door opener		
air conditioning		
television		
more than one television		
desktop computer		
laptop computer		
Internet access		
CD player		
cellular phone		

C   PREPARING TO READ

BACKGROUND

Bill Gates is the co-founder, chairman, and chief software architect of Microsoft© Corporation and one of the wealthiest people in the world. He has built a state-of-the-art home near Seattle, Washington. His home incorporates a variety of "Smart Home" technologies. A Smart Home is a home that has mechanical or electronic conveniences, many controlled by computers, that help make life easier and often save energy.

---

[1] *motion sensor lights:* lights that go on automatically when you enter a room or an area and go off when you leave

The picture below illustrates some Smart Home technologies. Guess what each mechanical or electronic device does in each room and write a few sentences describing it. Check your answers at the bottom of the page.

Smart Home: The house of tomorrow won't just shelter you and your family. It will take care of you.

VOCABULARY FOR COMPREHENSION

Guess the meaning of the underlined words from the context of the following sentences. Circle the letter of the word or phrase that is closest in meaning.

1. Some people can be very <u>ostentatious</u> about their technology: they like to have the latest technology only to impress their friends.
   a. smart
   b. quiet
   c. showy

2. Some technology is very <u>unobtrusive</u>. It can hardly be seen.
   a. loud
   b. modest
   c. modern

3. Smart Technology is interesting because it has the ability to <u>anticipate</u> your needs. For example, it knows when you are in a room and turns on the lights.
   a. expect
   b. ignore
   c. agree with

4. Smart Technology lighting is also able to sense when a room is <u>unoccupied</u> and turn off the lights.
   a. warm
   b. lighted
   c. empty

Answers: Ring the doorbell. Your picture appears on the TV screen, and the TV remote control opens the door. Open the garage door by remote control: the motion sensors turn on the lights. Use the telephone to turn on the stove or oven.

5. As you walk down a hallway in a Smart Home, you might not notice the lights ahead of you gradually going on and the lights behind you <u>fading</u>.
   a. changing colors
   b. going on
   c. disappearing

6. We are <u>confronted</u> by technology all the time. It is very difficult to get away from.
   a. met face to face with
   b. upset by
   c. confused by

7. Smart Home technology is <u>discreetly</u> displayed. For example, you might not even know that there is a television or computer in the room you are in!
   a. carefully
   b. openly
   c. never

8. Large wall-screens can display any picture, photo, or painting reproduction you choose from an enormous image database. The picture will <u>materialize</u> as you enter the room and disappear after you leave.
   a. stay
   b. appear
   c. exit

9. Not many people have <u>access</u> to the technology in Smart Homes now, but that will change over the next decade as the technology gets more popular and less expensive.
   a. the ability to obtain
   b. permission
   c. entry

10. In the end, Smart Home technology is smart and efficient, but do we want our homes to be run by computers and technology? If we do, let's hope we can <u>conceal</u> it, so we don't end up feeling like robots!
    a. destroy
    b. enlarge
    c. hide

2 Focus on Reading

A   READING ONE: *Inside the House*

Write a short answer to the following questions. Share your answer with a partner.

This reading describes Bill Gates's "dream house." What kind of a "dream house" would you want? Where would it be located? What five types of technology would you want in it? Do you think Bill Gates has them in his house?

_____

_____

_____

_____

_____

_____

_____

INSIDE THE HOUSE

BY BILL GATES
(from *The Road Ahead*)

1   I began thinking about building a new house in the late 1980s. I wanted craftsmanship but nothing ostentatious. I wanted a house that would accommodate sophisticated, changing technology, but in an unobtrusive way that made it clear that technology was the servant, not the master.

2   I found some property on the shore of Lake Washington within an easy commuting distance of Microsoft. Living space will be about average for a large house. The family living room will be about fourteen by twenty-eight feet, including an area for watching television or listening to music. And there will be cozy spaces for one or two people, although there will also be a reception hall to entertain one hundred comfortably for dinner.

3   First thing, as you come in, you'll be presented with an electronic pin to clip on your clothes. This pin will tell the home who and where you are, and the house will use this information to try to meet and even anticipate your needs—all as unobtrusively as possible. Someday, instead of needing the pin, it might be possible to have a camera system with visual-recognition capabilities,[1] but that's beyond current technology. When it's dark outside, the pin will cause a moving zone of light to

[1] *camera with visual-recognition capabilities:* a camera connected to a computer that can identify individual faces

accompany you through the house. Unoccupied rooms will be unlit. As you walk down a hallway, you might not notice the lights ahead of you gradually coming up to full brightness and the lights behind you fading. Music will move with you, too. It will seem to be everywhere, although, in fact, other people in the house will be hearing entirely different music or nothing at all. A movie or the news or a phone call will be able to follow you around the house, too. If you get a phone call, only the handset nearest you will ring.

4   You won't be confronted by[2] the technology, but it will be readily and easily available. Hand-held remote controls and discreetly visible consoles[3] in each room will put you in charge of your immediate environment and of the house's entertainment system. You'll use the controls to tell the monitors[4] in a room to become visible and what to display. You'll be able to choose from among thousands of pictures, recordings, movies, and television programs, and you'll have all sorts of options available for selecting information.

5   If you're planning to visit Hong Kong soon, you might ask the screen in your room to show you pictures of the city. It will seem to you as if the photographs are displayed everywhere, although actually the images will materialize on the walls of rooms just before you walk in and vanish after you leave. If you and I are enjoying different things and one of us walks into a room where the other is sitting, the house might continue the audio and visual imagery for the person who was in the room first, or it might change to programming both of us like.

[2] **be confronted by:** to have to deal with; to be forced to meet
[3] **console:** a cabinet or a case that holds a computer or television screen
[4] **monitor:** a computer or television screen

6   I will be the first home user for one of the most unusual electronic features in my house. The product is a database[5] of more than a million still images, including photographs and reproductions of paintings. If you are a guest, you'll be able to call up portraits of presidents, pictures of sunsets, airplanes, skiing in the Andes, a rare French stamp, the Beatles in 1965, or reproductions of High Renaissance paintings, on screens throughout the house.

7   I believe quality images will be in great demand on the information highway.[6] This vision that the public will find image-browsing worthwhile is obviously unproven. I think the right interface will make it appealing to a lot of people.

8   A decade from now, access to the millions of images and all the other entertainment opportunities I've described will be available in many homes and will certainly be more impressive than those I'll have when I move into my house. My house will just be getting some of the services a little sooner.

9   One of the many fears expressed about the information highway is that it will reduce the time people spend socializing. Some worry that homes will become such cozy entertainment providers that we'll never leave them, and that, safe in our private sanctuaries,[7] we'll become isolated. I don't think that's going to happen. As behaviorists[8] keep reminding us, we're social animals. We will have the option of staying home more because the highway will create so many new options for home-based entertainment, for communication—both personal and professional—and for employment. Although the mix of activities will change, I think people will decide to spend almost as much time out of their homes.

10   The highway will not only make it easier to keep up with distant friends, it will also enable us to find new companions. Friendships formed across the network will lead naturally to getting together in person. This alone will make life more interesting. Suppose you want to reach someone to play bridge with. The information highway will let you find card players with the right skill level and availability in your neighborhood, or in other cities or nations.

11   I enjoy experimenting, and I know some of my concepts for the house will work out better than others. Maybe I'll decide to conceal the monitors behind conventional wall art or throw the electronic pins into the trash. Or maybe I'll grow accustomed to the systems in the house, or even fond of them, and wonder how I got along without them. That's my hope.

---

[5] *database:* a large collection of information stored in a computer
[6] *information highway:* the Internet
[7] *sanctuary:* a safe and peaceful place
[8] *behaviorist:* a scientist who studies human behavior

READING FOR MAIN IDEAS

"Inside the House" can be divided into three main ideas. What does the reading say about each idea? Circle the letter of the sentence that summarizes the idea.

1. Description of the house
   a. Even though the house is larger than an average house, Bill Gates does not want it to feel cold or unfriendly.
   b. Bill Gates designed the house to accommodate 100 dinner guests.

2. Description of the technology in the house
   a. The technology is designed to be impressive and complex.
   b. The technology is designed to be easy to use and energy-efficient.

3. Analysis of the technology
   a. The information highway is a necessary part of everyone's life.
   b. Although the information highway has both positive and negative aspects, it is basically a positive technology.

READING FOR DETAILS

An outline is a visual guide that shows the main ideas, supporting ideas, examples, and further explanations of a text. Outlines are useful when taking notes from texts or when organizing essays. Some outlines are specific and show all the details; others are general. Below is an example of a detailed outline.

Complete the outline with the missing information from Reading One, including main ideas, supporting ideas, examples, and further explanations. Look back at the reading if you need help. When you have finished, compare outlines with a partner.

(main idea) **I. Thinking about home in the late 1980s**

(supporting idea) **A.** Style preferences

    (example) **1.** _____

    2. not ostentatious

  B. Must accommodate sophisticated and changing technology

    1. not obtrusive

    2. functions as servant, not master

II. Selecting the perfect property

  A. Location

    1. _____

    2. easy commuting distance

  B. Living space—average size

    1. living room

(further explanation) **a.** size = _____

    b. area for _____ or _____

       2. other cozy spaces for one or two people

       3. _____

          a. accommodates 100

III. Controlling the home environment with _____

    A. Tells the home _____ and _____

    B. House uses pin information to meet your needs

       1. _____ follows you

       2. _____ follows you

       3. _____ follows you

       4. _____ follows you

IV. Other readily and easily available technology

    A. Hand-held remotes and consoles in each room

    1. controls tell monitors

       a. _____

       b. _____

    B. Visual displays

    1. large choice

       a. thousands of pictures

       b. _____

       c. _____

       d. television programs

       e. many options for selecting information

    2. house can control visual displays

       a. materialize when you _____ and vanish when you _____

       b. house can change programming depending on _____

V. State-of-the-art database

    A. First homeowner to have it

    B. Database has more than _____

       1. includes photographs

       2. includes _____

    C. Guests can call up anything they like

       1. _____

       2. pictures of sunsets

       3. skiing in the Andes, etc.

VI. Future availability of quality images

    A. On the information highway

    B. In homes

VII. Fears about _____

    A. Reduces the time people spend socializing

        1. homes will become too cozy and self-contained

        2. people will become _____

    B. Not in agreement

        1. people are social animals

        2. highway only provides more entertainment and
           _____ options

           a. _____

           b. _____

           c. _____

        3. people will decide to spend as much time out of their homes

VIII. Benefits of the information highway

    A. Makes it easier to

        1. maintain _____

        2. find _____

    B. Makes life more interesting

        1. people will meet in person

        2. meet people with common interests

IX. Conclusion: Experimenting and the future

    A. Bill Gates enjoys experimenting and may decide to

        1. _____

        2. _____

    B. Hopes

        1. may like everything

        2. wonders how _____

REACTING TO THE READING

1 *The following opinions were not directly stated in the reading but can be inferred from it. Find an example from the reading that supports each inference. Note the paragraph where you found the support.*

    1. Technology should make life easier; it should not take over your life.

    Example: _____

    Paragraph: _____

2. A large home can be intimate.

Example: _____

Paragraph: _____

3. Homes should have energy-saving devices.

Example: _____

Paragraph: _____

4. A home should make guests feel comfortable by providing entertainment.

Example: _____

Paragraph: _____

5. The information highway allows people to be in the comfort of their home but, at the same time, stay connected to the world.

Example: _____

Paragraph: _____

6. The design of a home should be current but also allow for changes over time.

Example: _____

Paragraph: _____

2 *Discuss these questions in a small group. Share your ideas with the class.*

1. Critics believe that "one of the many fears expressed about the information highway is that it will reduce the time people spend socializing." What do you think? Has the Internet affected the time you spend socializing? Do you believe it is isolating or will it "create . . . many new options for home-based entertainment, for communication—both personal and professional—and for employment," as the reading said?

2. What is your reaction to Bill Gates's home? Do you find it appealing? Why or why not? Would you incorporate any of his ideas into your "dream house"? If so, which ones?

B READING TWO: *Thoreau's Home*

Henry David Thoreau was an American philosopher whose ideas inspired generations of readers to think for themselves and appreciate the ways of nature and humankind. In 1845, he moved to the woods of Massachusetts. He chose to live a life that reflected his philosophy: Live life in the simplest of ways. He did not believe luxuries or comforts were necessary; in fact, he felt they actually stopped human progress.

Discuss this question with a partner.

In what ways might technology actually stop or interfere with human progress?

THOREAU'S HOME

BY HENRY DAVID THOREAU
(edited, from *Walden*)

Thoreau's Home

1   Near the end of March 1845, I borrowed an axe and went down to the woods by Walden Pond[1] nearest to where I intended to build my house, and began to cut down some tall arrowy white pines, still in their youth, for timber.[2] . . . It was a pleasant hillside where I worked, covered with pine woods, through which I looked out on the pond, and a small open field in the woods where pines and hickories were springing up.[3] The ice on the pond was not yet dissolved, though there were some open spaces, and it was all dark colored and saturated with water. . . .

2   So I went on for some days cutting and hewing timber, and also studs and rafters,[4] all with my narrow axe, not having many communicable or scholar-like thoughts, singing to myself,

> Men say they know many things;
> But lo! they have taken wings—
> The arts and sciences,
> And a thousand appliances;
> The wind that blows
> Is all anybody knows.

---

[1] *Walden Pond:* a pond (area of fresh water) located in Concord, Massachusetts
[2] *timber:* wood used for building or making things
[3] *springing up:* growing
[4] *studs and rafters:* beams and pieces of wood that form the structure of a building

3   My days in the woods were not very long ones; yet I usually carried my dinner of bread and butter, and read the newspaper in which it was wrapped, at noon, sitting amid the green pine boughs which I had cut off, and to my bread was imparted some of their fragrance, for my hands were covered with a thick coat of pitch.[5] . . .

4   Before winter I built a chimney, and shingled the sides of my house, which were impervious to[6] rain. . . .

5   I have thus a tight shingled and plastered house, ten feet wide by fifteen feet long, and eight-feet posts, with a garret[7] and a closet, a large window on each side, two trap doors, one door at each end, and a brick fireplace opposite. The exact cost of my house, paying the usual price for such materials as I used, but not counting the work, all of which was done by myself, was as follows; and I give the details because very few are able to tell exactly what their houses cost, and fewer still, if any, the separate cost of the various materials which compose them:

Boards	$8.03½	Mostly shanty boards
Refuse shingles for roof and sides	4.00	
Laths	1.25	
Two second-hand windows with glass	2.43	
One thousand old bricks	4.00	
Two casks of lime	2.40	That was high.
Hair	0.31	More than I needed.
Mantle-tree iron	0.15	
Nails	3.90	
Hinges and screws	0.14	
Latch	0.10	
Chalk	0.01	
Transportation	1.40	I carried a good part on my back.
In all	$28.12½	

[5] *pitch:* sap from a pine tree
[6] *impervious to:* protected against
[7] *garret:* a small room at the top of a house

Work in a small group. Write short answers to these questions. Why do you think Thoreau wanted to build his own house? Was building his own home more satisfying than having someone else build it for him? If so, how?

C LINKING READINGS ONE AND TWO

Work with a partner. Imagine that one of you is Bill Gates and the other is Henry David Thoreau. Imagine you could write to each other and ask each other questions. What questions would you ask? For example: How big is your house? What luxuries do you have in your house? Write five questions and then exchange your questions with your partner. Write an answer to each question based on your understanding of Readings One and Two.

3 Focus on Vocabulary

1 *Complete the chart with the different forms of the words found in the readings. Not all of the words have all four forms. If you need help, use a dictionary.*

NOUN	VERB	ADJECTIVE	ADVERB
availability	X	available	*availably*
behaviorist			X
brightness	X		
		communicable	X
	X	conventional	
entertainment			X
friendship	X		X
information			
	materialize		X
	X	ostentatious	
television			X
	X	visible, visual	

2 *Complete the sentences with the correct form of the words given.*

1. **vision   entertainment**

   a. The monitors in Bill Gates's home will not be _____visible_____ until you turn them on.

   b. Bill Gates believes that one of the goals of technology is to

      _____ .

   c. _____ , however, is not the only goal of technology; improving the quality of life is also important.

   d. Bill Gates has many _____ for the future of technology.

   e. The use of _____-recognition cameras is one of Bill Gates's future plans.

2. **communication   information**

   a. Some of the data and facts are _____ and useful, but other information is just not true.

   b. Personal computers, modems, e-mail, and fax machines have increased the speed of _____ dramatically.

   c. Unfortunately, not all the _____ on the Internet is correct.

   d. One of the advantages of the information highway is that it allows people to _____ with co-workers without actually traveling to the office.

   e. Because Bill Gates's house was out of the ordinary, it was necessary for him to _____ the builders of exactly what he wanted.

3. **friendship   material**

   a. In a Smart Home your favorite pictures will _____ on the walls of the rooms just before you walk in.

   b. Some of Thoreau's contemporaries felt that he was not _____ because he often kept to himself.

   c. Thoreau used many reused _____ when building his home; this was part of his belief in living economically and simply.

   d. Bill Gates feels that the information highway can be used to foster

      _____ .

   e. Thoreau rejected the _____ world.

3 *Write responses to the following questions as Bill Gates or Henry David Thoreau. Use six to ten of the words from exercises 1 and 2 on pages 230–231.*

1. How would you describe your house to someone who has never seen it?
   Bill Gates:

   _____

   _____

   _____

2. How would you describe your house to someone who has never seen it?
   Henry David Thoreau:

   _____

   _____

   _____

3. What is your philosophy about the role of technology in life?
   Bill Gates:

   _____

   _____

   _____

4. What is your philosophy about the role of technology in life?
   Henry David Thoreau:

   _____

   _____

   _____

4 Focus on Writing

A   GRAMMAR: Future Progressive

1 *Read the following paragraph, and answer the questions with a partner.*

As technology advances, our lives <u>will be changing</u> day by day. In the future, more and more people <u>will be building</u> Smart Homes like Bill Gates's. People in general are <u>going to be using</u> technology more and more in their everyday lives.

We <u>will be using</u> the information highway for a wide range of activities such as home schooling, reading books, telecommuting, and taking virtual vacations. Our children certainly <u>won't be living</u> as we live; they will have many more electronic conveniences, but also some inconveniences. For example, today if we have a complaint or suggestion about some product or service, we are often able to make it to a "live" person. In the future, our children may not have this option. They probably <u>won't be complaining</u> to a person, but only to a machine. Although technological advances are designed to improve the quality of life, you <u>will be talking</u> about the "good old days" when life was simpler, just as your parents did before you. Technology may change our lifestyle but not our human nature. As the French say, the more things change, the more they stay the same!

1. Is the paragraph describing past, present, or future events?

2. Is the focus of the paragraph on the events themselves or on the fact that the events are ongoing?

Future Progressive

The **future progressive** tense is used to talk about actions that will be in progress at a specific time in the future. It is also used to emphasize the ongoing nature of the action.

Forming the Future Progressive

- The future progressive is formed with

  will (not) + **be** + base form + **-ing**

  OR

  be (not) going to + **be** + base form + **-ing**

  Tomorrow at 4:00, I **will be sending** an e-mail to friends in Colombia.

  I **won't be talking** on my cellular phone at that time.

  I'm going to be using the computer all day.

  I'm not going to be using my laptop computer in class.

- As with all progressive tenses, the future progressive is not usually used with non-action (stative) verbs.

  Bill Gates **will be** in New York at 6:00 P.M. tomorrow.
  (NOT *will be being*)

  (continued)

Future Progressive with Time Clauses

- If there is a time clause in the sentence, the time clause is in the simple present or the present progressive tense, not the future.

  He'**ll be flying** to Spain while the other executives **conclude** the conference.

  While the other executives **are concluding** the conference, he'**ll be flying** to Spain.

  GRAMMAR TIP: When a sentence begins with a dependent clause (the clause beginning with a time word), a comma separates it from the main clause. When a sentence begins with the main clause, no comma is necessary.

2 *Complete the following paragraph. Use the future progressive, but remember to use the present tense for the time clauses.*

Matt Olsen is a very busy man. Every day he has a full schedule. Tomorrow, for example, before he even eats breakfast, he'll ___be communicating___ with
1. (communicate)
associates in France in cyberspace. At 9:00 A.M. he _____
2. (meet)
with Microsoft development engineers. At 9:45 he _____
3. (try)
out a new version of "Windows XP." From 10:30 to 11:00 he

_____ letters to his secretary. After he
4. (dictate)
_____ to his wife on the phone, he _____
5. (talk)   6. (eat)
lunch with his plant manager. After lunch, he and his staff

_____ the visual-recognition capabilities of the new "smart
7. (test)
camera." Don't try calling him after 3:00 P.M., however, because he is going to be spending some time exercising in his personal gym. At 4:45 he

_____ back in his office. Before he _____
8. (be)   9. (eat)
dinner, he _____ to his Japanese business associates for
10. (talk)
about thirty minutes. For dinner, he _____ a fresh salad,
11. (have)
salmon steaks, and couscous. Remember not to call him after 10:00 P.M.

because he _____ . He certainly _____
12. (sleep)   13. (not wait)
for your call.

3 *Imagine that Mr. Sam Woodson, a high school history teacher, has been reading Henry David Thoreau's writing recently. He has decided to take a year off from his job and try to recreate some of Thoreau's famous trips and projects. Look at the tentative calendar he has planned for next year.*

Plans for Next Year			
JANUARY	**FEBRUARY**	**MARCH**	**APRIL**
Go on winter camping excursion in western Massachusetts	Visit Walt Whitman's home in New York	Build full-size model of cabin at Walden Pond	Walk the beaches of Cape Cod and write about experiences
MAY	**JUNE**	**JULY**	**AUGUST**
(Continue to) build full-size model of cabin at Walden Pond	Live in model of Walden pond cabin	Travel by boat on the Concord River	Study transcendentalist philosophy
SEPTEMBER	**OCTOBER**	**NOVEMBER**	**DECEMBER**
Take railroad from Concord, Massachusetts, to Bangor, Maine	Live in the back-woods of Maine	Travel by boat on the Merrimack River	Write about experiences following the footsteps of H. D. Thoreau

Sam had to make some changes in his schedule. The calendar below shows his final plans for next year.

Revised Plans for Next Year			
JANUARY	**FEBRUARY**	**MARCH**	**APRIL**
Visit Walt Whitman's home in New York	Go on winter camping excursion in western Massachusetts	Build full-size model of cabin at Walden Pond	(Continue to) build full-size model of cabin at Walden Pond
MAY	**JUNE**	**JULY**	**AUGUST**
Live in model of Walden pond cabin	Walk the beaches of Cape Cod and write about experiences	Travel by boat on the Concord River	Take railroad from Concord, Massachusetts, to Bangor, Maine
SEPTEMBER	**OCTOBER**	**NOVEMBER**	**DECEMBER**
Live in the back-woods of Maine	Travel by boat on the Merrimack River	Study transcendentalist philosophy	Write about experiences following the footsteps of H. D. Thoreau

Complete the sentences that follow using the information in both calendars. Be careful—the information given in each sentence reflects his tentative plans. Many of these plans have changed. Check the revised calendar carefully, and complete the sentences. Use the future progressive, but remember to use the present tense for the time clauses.

1. In January, Sam <u>won't be going on a winter camping excursion in western</u>
(go / winter camping excursion)
<u>Massachusetts. He will be visiting Walt Whitman's home in New York.</u>

2. In February, Sam _____
(visit / Walt Whitman's home in New York)

_____

_____

3. In March, Sam _____
(build / model of cabin)

_____

_____

4. In April, Sam _____
(walk / beaches of Cape Cod)

_____

_____

5. In May, Sam _____
(build / model of cabin)

_____

_____

6. In June, Sam _____
(live / model of Walden Pond cabin)

_____

_____

7. In July, Sam _____
(travel / boat on Concord River)

_____

_____

8. In August, Sam _____
(study / transcendentalist philosophy)

_____

_____

9. In September, Sam _____
(take / railroad from Concord, Massachusetts)

_____

_____

10. In October, Sam _____
    (live / backwoods of Maine)

    _____

    _____

11. In November, Sam _____
    (travel / boat on Merrimack River)

    _____

    _____

12. In December, Sam _____
    (write / experiences)

    _____

    _____

B STYLE: Outlines

1 *Work with a partner. Examine the following outline from part of Reading One. Then follow the instructions on page 238.*

_____ **I. Fears about the information highway**

     _____ **A.** Reduces the time people spend socializing

         _____ **1.** homes will become too cozy and self-contained

         _____ **2.** people will stay home more and become isolated

     _____ **B.** Not in agreement

         _____ **1.** people are social animals

         _____ **2.** highway only provides more entertainment and communication options

             _____ **a.** personal

             _____ **b.** professional

             _____ **c.** employment

         _____ **3.** people will decide to spend just as much time out of their homes

_____ **II. Benefits of the information highway**

     _____ **A.** Makes it easier to

         _____ **1.** maintain distant relationships

         _____ **2.** find new companions

     _____ **B.** Makes life more interesting

         _____ **1.** people will meet in person

         _____ **2.** meet people with common interests

1. Label the main ideas (MI).

2. Label the supporting ideas (SI).

3. Label the examples (E).

4. Label the further explanations (FE).

5. Find the paragraph in Reading One that describes fears about the information highway. How does the outline reflect this paragraph?

Outlines

An **outline** helps you organize your notes or ideas before you begin to write. It helps you see the order in which you will talk about the main ideas, and it guides you in selecting details and examples to support those ideas. An outline shows you where to add more details, give more examples, or change the order of the main points. Preparing and following an outline is a useful prewriting activity.

The Structure of an Outline

An outline is usually written in the following way:

    I. Main idea (can also be written as a topic sentence)

(indent) **A.** Supporting idea 1 (supports the topic sentence)

  (indent) **1.** example (exemplifies the supporting detail)

      2. example

   (indent) **a.** further explanation (exemplifies the example)

      b. further explanation

    B. Supporting idea 2 (supports the topic sentence)

      1. example (exemplifies the supporting detail)

        a. further explanation (exemplifies the example)

      2. example

        a. further explanation (exemplifies the example)

      b. further explanation

Outline writing can be a useful tool for taking notes in order to summarize information. Your ideas do not have to be complete sentences, although some people like to write the main idea as a topic sentence. Some outlines are quite simple: They list only the main ideas (I, II) and a few supporting ideas (A, B). Some outlines are more detailed: They include many main ideas (I, II, III, IV), supporting ideas (A, B, C, D), examples (1, 2, 3, 4), and further explanations (a, b, c, d).

2 *Read the last paragraph and chart of "Thoreau's Home" and complete the outline.*

    I. The house is efficient in size and economical.

      A. Size and description

        1. ten feet wide by fifteen feet long

        2. _____

        3. garret and closet

        4. _____

        5. two trap doors

        6. _____

        7. brick fireplace

      B. Economical construction

        1. work done himself

        2. total cost $28.12½

3 *Write a complete three-paragraph essay following the outline below. Be sure to include a topic sentence, supporting sentences, supporting ideas, and a concluding sentence. (See Unit 1, pages 18 and 19, and Unit 2, pages 41 and 42, for review.)*

    I. Technology has done many wonderful things for us.

      A. Sciences

        1. better health care

        2. healthier food preservation

      B. Communication

        1. people you know

        2. people you don't know

      C. Comforts

        1. television

        2. computers

    II. Technology also has many negative sides.

      A. Acid rain from cars and industry

        1. affects 45 percent of lakes in Sweden

        2. costs millions of dollars to repair damage

      B. Interpersonal relations

        1. loss of face-to-face contact

        2. decline in traditional writing skills as e-mail becomes more common

III. **We need to produce "Smart Technology" that makes our lives better without damaging the environment.**

    A. Research groups

        1. produce useful research and Smart Technology

        2. maintain funding for innovative technology

    B. Educate our citizens

        1. start in elementary schools

        2. encourage young people to think about the difference between wasteful and dangerous technology and Smart Technology

C | WRITING TOPICS

Write an essay about one of these topics. Before you write, make an outline. Be sure to use some of the ideas, vocabulary, grammar, and style that you have learned in this unit.

1. Thoreau wrote, "Our life is frittered away by detail. An honest man has hardly need to count more than his ten fingers, or in extreme cases he may add his ten toes, and lump the rest. Simplicity, simplicity, simplicity!" Thoreau felt that we need only a simple life without modern comforts and technology to appreciate the world around us. Do you agree or disagree? Explain your answer.

2. Imagine you have to eliminate five technological devices from your life. What would they be? What, if anything, would you replace them with? How would your life be different?

3. Technology is necessary to help people live longer and better. Many people believe it would be impossible to live without technology. Do you agree or disagree? Explain your answer.

4. When is technology a necessity? When is technology a luxury? Does the definition of a luxury change over time? In other words, are some things that were thought of as luxuries 10, 20, or 100 years ago now considered necessities? Explain your answer.

5. How has the Internet changed your life? Think about both the positive and negative impact the Internet has had on you. Address the benefits and drawbacks, and the freedoms and limitations using that the Internet brings.

D RESEARCH TOPIC

Report on the role technology has had in your life.

Step 1: Think about what technological devices and machines you have now that did not exist when you were younger. How has technology changed the quality of your life? Complete the following chart. When you are finished, share it with a partner.

WHAT I USED AS A CHILD OR YOUNG PERSON	WHAT HAS REPLACED IT	HOW IT HAS CHANGED THE QUALITY OF MY LIFE
Books, library	Internet	I'm able to get information faster and more easily. It also saves a lot of time. On the other hand, I stay at home more and never go to the library or bookstore.

Step 2: Interview an older person (for example, a teacher, friend, or relative from another generation) about the changes he or she has seen in technology during his or her lifetime. Use the chart above as a guide. Write a report including answers to the following questions. Add at least three more of your own questions. Present your report to the class.

- In your opinion, what is the most significant technological advance in your lifetime? Why do you think so?

- What technological advance has affected you most personally? How has it changed your life?

- _____

- _____

- _____

For step-by-step practice in the writing process, see the *Writing Activity Book, High Intermediate,* Unit 10.

Assignment	Comparison and contrast essay
Prewriting	Identifying effective prewriting techniques
Organizing	Analyzing the topic and outlining your ideas
Revising	Choosing effective supporting ideas
	Making predictions with the future progressive
Editing	Correcting parallel structure

For Unit 10 Internet activities, visit the NorthStar Companion Website at
http://www.longman.com/northstar

Grammar Book References

NorthStar: Reading and Writing, High Intermediate, Second Edition	Focus on Grammar, High Intermediate, Second Edition	Azar's Understanding and Using English Grammar, Third Edition
Unit 1 Passive Voice	**Unit 18** The Passive: Overview	**Chapter 11** The Passive: 11-1, 11-2
Unit 2 Gerunds and Infinitives	**Unit 9** Gerunds and Infinitives: Review and Expansion	**Chapter 14** Gerunds and Infinitives, Part 1 **Chapter 15** Gerunds and Infinitives, Part 2
Unit 3 Past Unreal Conditionals	**Unit 24** Unreal Conditionals: Past	**Chapter 20** Conditional Sentences and Wishes: 20-1, 20-4
Unit 4 Identifying Adjective Clauses	**Unit 13** Adjective Clauses with Subject Relative Pronouns **Unit 14** Adjective Clauses with Object Relative Pronouns or *When* and *Where*	**Chapter 13** Adjective Clauses
Unit 5 Advisability and Obligation in the Past	**Unit 16** Advisability and Obligation in the Past	**Chapter 9** Modals, Part 1: 9-7, 9-8, 9-11
Unit 6 Tag Questions	**Unit 7** Negative *Yes/No* Questions and Tag Questions	**Appendix** Unit B: Questions: B-5
Unit 7 Direct and Indirect Speech	**Unit 25** Direct and Indirect Speech	**Chapter 12** Noun Clauses: 12-6, 12-7

NorthStar: Reading and Writing, High Intermediate, Second Edition	Focus on Grammar, High Intermediate, Second Edition	Azar's Understanding and Using English Grammar, Third Edition
Unit 8 Phrasal Verbs	**Unit 11** Phrasal Verbs: Review **Unit 12** Phrasal Verbs: Separable and Inseparable	**Appendix** Unit E: Preposition Combinations See also Appendix 1: Phrasal Verbs in *Fundamentals of English Grammar, Third Edition*
Unit 9 Past Perfect	**Unit 4** Past Perfect and Past Perfect Progressive	**Chapter 3** Perfect and Perfect Progressive Tenses: 3-3
Unit 10 Future Progressive	**Unit 5** Future and Future Progressive	**Chapter 4** Future Time: 4-5

Credits

Notes

Notes

Notes

Notes

Notes

Notes

Notes

NORTHSTAR   CD Tracking Guide

CD 1

1. Audio Program Introduction

UNIT 1

2. Reading One
3. Reading Two

UNIT 2

4. Reading One
5. Reading Two

UNIT 3

6. Reading One
7. Reading Two

UNIT 4

8. Reading One
9. Reading Two

UNIT 5

10. Reading One
11. Reading Two

CD 2

1. Audio Program Introduction

UNIT 6

2. Reading One
3. Reading Two

UNIT 7

4. Reading One
5. Reading Two

UNIT 8

6. Reading One
7. Reading Two

UNIT 9

8. Reading One
9. Reading Two

UNIT 10

10. Reading One
11. Reading Two